EMPOWERED TO UPGRADE

The Ultimate Guide to Taking Control of Your Career with Confidence

SHANNON D. SMITH

PUBLISHER

Career Essentials Press

Woodbridge, Virginia, US

Contents

Get Your Free Gift!

As a token of my appreciation for purchasing this book, I am offering you the audiobook for free! All you need to do is go to empoweredtoupgrade.com/audio to download it now!

Introduction

If you're reading this book, it's probably because you feel stuck in your career. You carry a sinking feeling in the pit of your stomach on Sundays because you know what the next holds...work that doesn't excite you...a job that doesn't light you up. Stress, a terrible boss, a disappointing paycheck, and difficult co-workers, just to name a few are also waiting for you. Perhaps you've convinced yourself that this is just the way it has to be. You have to pay bills, right? I know exactly how you feel. I spent years feeling unfulfilled and uncertain in my career until I finally took a chance on myself to proactively pursue what I wanted to do. It was the best decision I ever made, and I want to help you do the same.

Take a moment to think about when you first started your career. Were you enthusiastic? Did you consider all the possibilities? I bet you set your sights on reaching the top of your industry with excitement so you could make more money, while making a difference. Yet, for many there comes a point where the job stops feeling like a dream. This is when most people become uninspired. They check out mentally and feel stuck, coasting every day and counting down the seconds to 5pm. Many reasons drive us to dissatisfaction in our career. Sometimes it's money, a position that is not growing anywhere, outdated skills, or boredom in the work we are doing. Whatever has you unhappy or dissatisfied, you have the right book. Life is too short to spend your days doing something you don't enjoy. It's time to take control of your career and make a change! My goal is to help you shift into a career that aligns with who you are, puts a spring in your step, more money in your pocket and joy in your Monday mornings.

You may be wondering, if so many people are unhappy in their career, why won't they just make a change? That definitely makes sense, but for some, change is easier said than done. Our brains are wired to resist change so it can be a challenge. Fear and uncertainty also play a part because, like me years ago, I didn't know where to start. To ensure you are empowered to upgrade your career, you will need to upgrade your mindset, skills, and strategies, which are essential. I've learned that failing to proactively manage your career can leave you underpaid, underemployed and unfulfilled. Not to mention the feelings of overwhelm, frustration, and hopelessness about the outlook of your future. I don't want this to be you. I want you to use this book to take control of your career and live powerfully. I want you to discover who you really are so you can align who you are with what you do. Are you ready to make the shift from passive to powerful in your career? I hope so, because

I'm ready to receive your testimonials and stories of how you finally took your power back, went after your dreams, and achieved them. I want to cry tears of joy for you and celebrate your breakthroughs. Will you give me that gift, my friend? If you're saying yes, reading so we can get started!

WHAT THIS BOOK IS ABOUT

Empowered to Upgrade is a career empowerment blueprint for those who are tired of play small and living beneath their potential. This book is packed with actionable advice, inspiring stories, and encouragement that will show you how to tap into your personal power so you can take control of your career. All it takes is an upgrade, which includes having the right mindset, skills, and strategies in place to see your dreams come true. I believe we should all have the choice and opportunity to work and live in the way we choose. With this book in your hand, you'll be able to move forward with in your career pursuits with powerful confidence.

By the end of this book, you will walk away embracing these six core beliefs:

- I was created for more than earning a paycheck.

- I was created to make a difference in the lives of others.

- No one is coming to save me, therefore if it is to be, it is up to me.

- I have valuable talents, ideas and gifts that need to be shared with the world.

- Everything I need to succeed is within me. I just need the right mindset, skills, and environment to thrive.

- I am ready to stop playing small; sitting on the sidelines of life while others around me get in the game.

If you are ready to do the work to live by these beliefs, then my friend, you're in the right place, with the right book! I am so excited to partner with you on a wonderful journey of growth!

WHO THIS BOOK IS NOT FOR

This book is not for people who are content with playing small and living beneath their potential. If you are unwilling to embrace change or would rather listen to fear instead of listening to your heart, this book is not for you.

SECTION I:

SHIFTING FROM PASSIVE TO POWERFUL

CHAPTER 1:

PASSIVE = PASSED OVER!

"Growth is an active process that is intentional, demands energy and determination, while death is passive and effortless demands nothing from us. However, they are both natural phenomena that we have to choose as they war against each other in our lives." – Dr. Lucas D. Shallua

People everywhere wait for something good to happen to them. Some are waiting for their talents to be discovered, to be seen, heard, and appreciated. Some are waiting for a raise, a promotion, a pat on the back, or validation of their value. I know because I was one of those people. I sat on the sidelines of life waiting to be noticed. I often hoped one day someone would see me for who I was, and the gifts I had to offer. What I longed for was external validation and approval. Years later, I learned a valuable lesson: as long as I waited for someone else to see me, validate me, or give me "permission" to do what was in my heart to do, I'd wait forever and miss my opportunity to fulfill my purpose. The good we all desire to achieve or receive does not happen while we wait. It happens when we take intentional, consistent action aligned with our values and who we are. When we stay passive, we get passed over. It is not until we decide to shift into our personal power that we attract the good we desire and experience the life we deserve.

Let's define what it means to be passive. The Oxford dictionary defines it as "accepting or allowing what happens or what others do, without active response or resistance." In what areas of your career are you simply allowing things to happen without response or resistance? Are you allowing others to take credit for your work without speaking up? Are you allowing your organization to deny you a raise without negotiating? Are you allowing toxic co-workers or bosses to negatively impact your mental health without doing something about it? The challenge with being passive is that it robs you of your voice, identity, and choices. You forfeit your right to decide how you will be treated and what you will receive and experience. Passivity in essence tells everyone around you that their desires and needs are more important and yours are irrelevant. We betray ourselves when we choose to remain passive by failing to be our own advocate and therefore allowing others to advance their agenda in our lives.

Why are some people passive? Being passive can be the result of a character trait, a strategy to cope with difficult situations, or the byproduct of negative beliefs about ourselves. This is behavior that keeps you stuck in your career and prevents you from reaching your goals. When you're passive, you don't take risks and don't embrace change. You wait for things to happen, instead of making them happen. This can keep you stuck in a job you hate or prevent you from reaching new levels in your career. Being passive will also keep you from developing your personal power. Personal power gives you the ability to create change in your career and evolve into the best version of yourself.

In the corporate arena, we can't afford to be passive. We cannot allow ourselves to believe the myth that says if we just keep our heads down and work hard, we'll be rewarded, promoted, or given a raise. Believing this lie will have you waiting for an eternity to get the payoff you want. Those who get what they want, make it happen. They position themselves to be seen, valued, and heard. Taking this stance doesn't require you to be rude, arrogant, or obnoxious. But it does require you to be strategic and take intentional action. You will need to upgrade your mindset, skills, and strategies if you ever hope to shift from passive to powerful. You will also need to upgrade your self-perception. Failing to see ourselves as we truly are allows others to define us. It gives them an all-access pass to leverage our talents, skills, and abilities for their benefit rather than our own.

I am here to be your guide so you can avoid that detrimental mistake. If you are tired of being held prisoner by the inability to say no, finally advocate for your best interests, or increase your confidence, you are ready for an upgrade. It is in your best interests to develop a habit of self-advocacy if you intend to get in the driver's seat of your career and beyond. The journey from passive to powerful won't be easy, but it will definitely be worth it. Choose to live intentionally and take control of your career.

MY JOURNEY FROM PASSIVE TO POWERFUL

I have personally made the journey out of the wilderness of passivity into the land of personal power. What is beautiful about this journey is it continues, even now, so you have the opportunity to come along side me on this life affirming and empowering path. My decision to embrace my upgrade was the best decision I ever made. I am living proof that you don't have to remain passive, get passed over, and accept things as they are. I recall being a typical happy child. I loved humming and singing which would get me in trouble around dinner time. Singing was not allowed at the table. I also remember being tapped on my leg by my dad for humming and singing to myself in church. I had an uncontainable joy. That all changed around the age of seven. My mom left my dad and took us to Georgia. That year was the worst time in my life. I believe passivity set in during this period. I've learned that we become passive when we believe we have no control over our circumstances and therefore there is no use in trying to change anything. At seven years old I witnessed horrible things, cried nightly, and acted out because I wanted to return to some semblance of the normal life I remembered. When my actions did not impact my situation, it sowed a seed of negative belief within me that said there was no use in speaking up. No one would listen. I began a lifelong journey of suffering in silence instead. My adolescent and adulthood passivity were more progressive versions of what began in my childhood. During my time in school, I was very withdrawn, quiet, and rarely spoke to anyone. If I made friends, it was because someone else initiated it. What was also challenging about this time period was my extremely low self-esteem and poor self-image. Conditions such as these reinforced my passivity. It caused me to constantly rely on outside validation and the opinions of others to help me feel good about myself and be able to make decisions.

The turning point came years later. It was the summer of 2010. I was deeply depressed by my financial situation and the effects of leaving a ten-year abusive marriage. My friend invited me to a birthday party to lift my spirits. I reluctantly attended the party. When I got home, I discovered that someone had broken into my home by shattering the glass patio door with a brick. My room was ransacked and the little I had was stolen. I felt so violated and angry! Once again, someone was able to do whatever they wanted to me without consequence. The children were scared and crying. Looking at their little faces at ages 1, 2, 10, and 12 shattered my heart like the brick had shattered the glass door. I felt completely helpless because I was so bad off financially that I could not afford to get a hotel room that night. It was the worst night of my life as a mother. I felt like a complete failure. Thankfully, my friend and her husband stayed overnight and helped me sort things out.

Throughout the night, I did some serious soul searching to answer the question we often ask ourselves in situations like this, "How did I get here?" Some astonishing revelations came to me. The biggest one was that I was allowing life to happen to me rather than determining what I wanted from life. I was not living intentionally. That was my breakthrough moment. I vowed to do everything in my power to stop letting life happen to me and do everything in my power live with intention. The next morning, I dug deeper into this thought and took time to really evaluate myself and how I planned to turn things around. This involved evaluating my thinking, beliefs, habits, and career. I realized that for my situation to change, I had to change first. Coming to that conclusion helped me see that I had to take personal responsibility for my life. In the area of thinking, I had a lot of negative self-talk that emphasized what I could not do, reasons why I was not better off, and what wasn't working. I harbored so much anger about not getting support from my ex-husband for our children that I lost sight of working on me. I have learned over the years that we get more of what we focus on. The more I focused on lack and limitations, the more lack and limits I experienced. It blinded me to the possibilities and opportunities around me. The fact that I hadn't worked on myself was also showing up in the way I conducted job searches and interviews, which was another factor keeping me from the income and career I wanted. It dawned on me that I was keeping my family from the quality of life we deserved. I must admit, that was a tough pill to swallow. Yet, it was needed. Honest self-reflection is what it takes to make any significant improvements in our lives.

After taking a personal inventory, I let go of anger and the things I couldn't control. Then I asked myself what my next step was going to be. I decided to complete my undergraduate degree, which I had put on pause during my marriage. This accomplishment improved my self-confidence greatly and bumped up my earning power slightly, but it wasn't enough. I continued my education and obtained a master's degree shortly afterwards. I became obsessed with self-improvement and self-empowerment, which has gotten me to where I am today. The break-in wake-up call, as I like to call it, was instrumental in helping me shift from a passive person who was letting life happen, to a powerful woman who is taking control of my future and changing my life. Now, I have a successful career and I established my own coaching practice, and podcast. I know firsthand how to turn career frustrations into career elevation. Learning how to create a career I love and income streams outside of my job was the best thing I could have done for myself. I believe lessons are meant to be shared, so I decided to put them in this book so you can achieve your own version of a career upgrade.

Life is too short to be miserable and live at the mercy of others. You should not give up on your dream of doing work that makes you look forward to getting up every morning. What many fail to realize is satisfaction and happiness starts within. Did you know that in most cases, job dissatisfaction is the result of poor job-fit, which means the work isn't aligned with a person's values, talents and strengths? My goal is to inspire you to get in the driver's seat of your career by equipping you the resources to make intentional decisions that lead to greater career satisfaction. Helping clients upgrade their mindset and career strategies is the foundation of the work I do. When frustrated people reach out to me because they're unhappy with their jobs, we work together to address their challenges, evaluate their personal brand, develop an entrepreneurial outlook towards their career, and focus on developing marketable skills. By the time we're done, my clients are the Chief Empowered Owner of their career. That's what I want for you, too! When it comes to experiencing frustration and overwhelm in your job, here is what I recommend before you make a rash decision: Regulate your emotions. Evaluate your situation and figure out how you got there. Decide what you need and want. Create a plan to get you to your goal and move at YOUR pace. Remember, comparison is the thief of joy, and I believe it can also lead many people to take premature action. The good news is from now on, you will take action that aligns with who you are, what you want, and where you want to be.

YOUR JOURNEY FROM PASSIVE TO POWERFUL

Your journey from passive to powerful is really about embracing change. For many of us, change is scary and uncomfortable. Our brains are wired to resist change because it sees it as a threat and wants to keep us safe in the comfort of familiarity. In order for you to embrace your upgrade and transform into a more powerful version of yourself who takes charge of your career, a decision has to be made. You're at a crossroad right now. So, do you stay where you are, comfortable, uninspired, unchallenged, and unfulfilled? Or do you face the unfamiliar, take a chance on yourself and go down the road less traveled?

If you choose to go with me on the path less traveled, the remainder of this book will be your guide. The good news is you don't have to do any of this alone. I know what it's like to feel trapped by a job you can't stand, yet bills that demanded you stay. You don't have to stay there. It's time to get you out of your rut into an empowered position that will bring you the alignment and career satisfaction you've been looking for! If you are serious about taking control of where your career is going, buckle up, we're going on a journey! You're about to get into the driver's seat of your career and take the wheel. Ready to embrace your upgrade? Keep reading!

Section II:

The UPGRADE Method

CHAPTER 2:

UPDATE YOUR MINDSET

"Our brains are like computers; it's our responsibility to programme them well daily and remove the viruses." – Sam Owen

Your mindset is a collection of your thoughts and beliefs. Your thinking affects your life because it influences your behavior, and habits, which determines what you get out of life. It is responsible for what you perceive as possible for you. For example, when I worked as a customer service representative, one of the things I often said to myself was "I never get promoted, why try". What type of behavior do you think this led to? I'll tell you, it led to mediocre performance which led to a self-fulfilling prophecy of not getting promoted. There is a psychology term for this, it's called confirmation bias which says our brains scan our environments to "confirm" our beliefs. So, in reality, we don't believe what we see, but rather we see what we believe. We all see possibility through the lens of our belief in our capabilities.

In order to improve anything, we must first understand how it comes to be. So, let's look at how we develop our mindsets. From 0-7 years of age, we are mental sponges because we operate only from our subconscious mind during this phase. We absorb information from our environment which includes schooling, family, and culture, without the ability to evaluate its accuracy. These environments inform us on what is acceptable and unacceptable. They also inform us on how we should view ourselves. We accept everything we see and hear as true. Once we hit 8, a switch is flipped in our mind, and we start operating from a conscious mind. Everything we absorbed from 0-7 years old becomes our belief system about ourselves and the world around us. From there we filter everything through this belief system, whether it is true or not. I'm sure you and I can both agree that not all the information we have come to believe about ourselves and the world around us is one-hundred percent accurate. I know for me, I had to undo a lot of faulty beliefs that reinforced negative thinking patterns and low self-esteem. I discovered the things I accepted to be truth as a child, such as words from bullies or ill-tempered words spoken by family members in moments of stress, were only opinions. Those words did not reflect who I was or who I would become. It also did not hold any insights into my potential. Coming to that realization was one of many life changing moments for me. I hope it will be helpful for you. You do not have to accept any belief that no longer serves or supports you. From now on, you get to decide what you believe about yourself, your capabilities, and your future. I hope it encourages you to know that you can update your old programming! It will require the intentional effort of upgrading your mindset. Your mindset includes your thinking, your beliefs, and your emotions. Updating these three will lead to an upgrade in your habits, expectations, and experiences, which will lead to achieving your career goals.

YOUR THINKING

One lesson I have learned is that everything you want to achieve starts with your mind. Napoleon Hill says, "Whatever the mind can conceive and believe, it can achieve." Your mindset is responsible for what you perceive as possible for you, and it will determine how successful you are in any pursuit. Your thoughts shape your life because they influence your behavior and impact your experiences. For example, if you think you are bad at your job, you won't perform quality work, and this will cause you to be overlooked for raises or promotions. These experiences will then reinforce your original thought. The psychology term for this is confirmation bias. It means our brains scan our environments to "confirm" our thoughts or beliefs. Rather than believing what we see, we actually see what we believe. An essential part of growth involves removing unhelpful thought patterns we have developed since childhood and learning to install new thoughts to help us become who we want to be.

BEST PRACTICES FOR UPGRADING YOUR THINKING

The following are some best practices for upgrading your thinking. The practices I will share really turned things around for me and I believe they can help you, as well. How often and at what intensity you use these practices is up to you.

MEDITATION

Meditation is the best kind of practice for improving your thinking. It involves sitting quietly and observing your thoughts. After a period of time, the mind starts to quiet down. You will feel a sense of calm sweep over you, and you will become less reactive to distractions. You will be able to monitor and control your thoughts efficiently. The benefits of meditation have been verified by science and many high-performing individuals engage in the practice. Meditation has historic roots in spiritual systems. Twice a day; preferably in the morning and evening for 20 minutes is the recommended timeframe for the best results. Don't worry if you can't do 20 minutes right away. Do what you can and work your way up. I personally started with 5 minutes because I have a very active mind. I gradually added minutes until I could sit quietly for 20 minutes.

PRACTICE GRATITUDE

A mind that focuses on what is missing in life will always see problems, but a mind that focuses on gratitude will always see possibilities. Even when things are not going well in your life, looking for the positive and focusing on what you are thankful for will help you feel optimistic about your future. Integrating gratitude into your daily routine does not have to be complicated. When you wake up, think of something you're thankful for. By beginning your day in gratitude, you create a positive state of mind before you get out of bed. You can also choose to write a gratitude list in a journal, as I do, or simply share with someone the things you are grateful for. I prefer writing because it gives me a record I can reflect on later. Choose what works for you. Making gratitude a regular practice will definitely shift your thinking. Your world will become more positive, and so will you.

PRACTICE MINDFULNESS

Mindfulness has positive health benefits such as stress reduction. The practice enhances your resilience and improves your mental capacity. Mindfulness means bringing your complete attention to the present, where you are right now, not distracted by memories of the past or anxieties about the future. Mindfulness brings you into a deeper connection with yourself and others. It gives you time and mental space to work out your values and beliefs. Living a life aligned with your values encourages and supports your inner wellbeing. One other beautiful effect of mindfulness is that you learn happiness lies in knowing yourself and being comfortable with who you are. You can use the 3 breaths technique to anchor your awareness firmly in the present to practice mindfulness. It's so easy you can do it right now as you're reading this. Simply bring your attention to your breath – breathe in slowly and gently, following the path of your breath with your mind. Feel it deep in your belly. Then breathe out slowly and gently, again, paying attention to the movement of your breath. Can you feel a subtle energy shift, a calm peacefulness? That is how mindfulness feels. Make a conscious decision to disconnect from distractions and focus your awareness on what you can see, feel, hear, smell and taste. This simple exercise will ground you in the present moment to experience mindfulness.

FOCUS ON HOW FAR YOU'VE COME

It is a mistake to measure your success by how close you are to your goals. A better approach is to measure your success by how far you've come from where you were. When I reflect on the times I had to rely on government assistance or take public transportation to get to work because I didn't have a car, versus where I am now; working from home, homeschooling my son, and loving the work I do, I feel a profound sense of pride and accomplishment. This motivates and inspires me to take more action because I am reminding myself of what I am capable of. Failing to do this can cause you to procrastinate and become demotivated because you're focusing on how far you have to go. Boost your motivation by focusing your thoughts on achievements so you can keep moving forward.

YOUR BELIEF

Your belief is the result of your thinking and your acceptance of a thought, statement, or circumstance as true. Pause and consider what you believe about your career, your potential, and your future. Did you know that the way you talk to yourself reflects your belief about who you are and what you are capable of? In addition to that, what you focus on impacts your beliefs. If your beliefs are not empowering you, they are limiting you. Limiting beliefs are negative, self-defeating thoughts that keep you from stepping out of your comfort zone and reaching your potential. Some examples of limiting beliefs are. "I'm not good enough." "No one will listen to me." "I don't have what it takes." Often, we accept these beliefs without challenging them. I've learned through lots of self-work to ask myself if a thought is true when limiting beliefs rear their ugly head. I search for evidence that the thought is true. In most cases I cannot find any evidence, so I look for evidence of the opposite. That's when I realize I have more working in my favor than against me. So, if a negative or limiting belief comes across your mind, ask yourself, "Is this true?" "Do I have evidence to prove this thought?" If you can't find any, dismiss the thought and replace it with the truth, which is that you are capable of figuring anything out, you were wired to learn new things, and you can accomplish the goals you set your mind to if you persevere.

Early in my career I was very shy. I believed everyone else had special talents, and somehow, I was overlooked by my creator. So, needless to say, I struggled with confidence. However, when I went on interviews, I answered questions in a way that contradicted what I believed about myself. The psychology term for this is cognitive dissonance. I may have answered the questions correctly, but my eyes, posture, tone, and facial expressions were telling the truth. Our body language always betrays us. It wasn't until I sought the help of a Neurolinguistic Programming (NLP) Coach that I realized my subconscious beliefs were running the show, instead of what I was consciously saying. I learned how to uncover the hidden belief and replace it with the truth. Once I accomplish that, I had alignment with what I was saying and believing. It made all the difference! From that point on, I interviewed with confidence and saw a drastic change in the amount of job offers I received.

Unfortunately, many people operate on autopilot so long that they don't know what they believe or why they do what they do. It's like sleepwalking through life. Sometimes it takes an unfortunate event to wake them up, as in my case, to force them to evaluate their lives. In hindsight, I'm grateful for my wake-up call. It shook me up enough to turn off autopilot and pushed me into problem solving mode. It also motivated me to reach out for help, mentorship, and knowledge. This was a huge turning point for me and was instrumental in boosting my belief in myself and changing my life.

CREATE A NEW BELIEF SYSTEM

To create a new belief system, you need affirmations and mantras. Affirmations are an effective tool to program ourselves for success. When affirming, remember to use the present tense. For example, "I am talented" or "I am rich" is better than "I will be talented" or "I am going to be rich." I recommend looking at yourself in the mirror when saying your affirmations. You can use affirmations like these; "I cannot fail, I either win or learn.", "Money flows to me often and with ease.", "I am becoming a________" (fill-in-the-blank), "I am becoming a person who______" (fill-in-the-blank), and " I don't know everything I need to know, but I can always figure it out."

Keep in mind that affirmations work best when the mind is in a receptive state. So, the best time for affirmations is first thing in the morning or late at night. Another time to repeat your affirmations is during meditation when they can really sink in without resistance. Also, if you can make your affirmations rhyme, your subconscious will repeat it consistently, like how a song gets stuck in your head. This is the best approach if you have a negative belief you want to get rid of. Where possible, try to feel your affirmation as a positive emotion. This supercharges it with energy and helps it to become a reality. Before you know it, you won't recognize yourself! You'll be the person you envisioned, and you will think, believe, and feel differently.

Mantras are words or phrases that you repeat to yourself in order to focus your thoughts and achieve a desired outcome. They can be used for anything from increasing productivity, improving self-confidence, or simply calming the mind and body. Mantras come from many different spiritual traditions but >can be adapted to any belief system or lifestyle. The important thing is to find a mantra that resonates with you on a personal level and then use it regularly to help guide your thoughts and actions.. Mantras help you reject negative thoughts by concentrating on positive words or phrases.

By using mantras, your thoughts will become clear, and negative thoughts will gradually become less frequent. The key is to speak your mantras consistently. The more personalized your mantras are, the more effective they become. Some examples are: "I am in control of my career.", "I am powerful and capable." And "I can do this!"

YOUR EMOTIONS

We all know that emotions play a huge role in our lives. But what many of us don't realize is how much they can hold us back – both professionally and personally. In fact, emotions are often the root of the bad habits that keep us from achieving our goals. How you feel is determined by the meaning you assign to circumstances and the behavior of others. Emotions are also born out of what you believe. For instance, I used to believe I was insignificant at work. So, when I wasn't called upon for special projects or acknowledged for certain contributions, I felt overlooked, rejected, and insignificant. My belief was the lens that I used to interpret people's facial expressions, tone of voice, and actions. I only saw what I believed, and therefore I continued to experience emotions that reinforced those beliefs. It became a vicious cycle of defeatism and despondency. Thankfully, seeking help allowed me to break the cycle and form new beliefs that allowed me to feel a different set of emotions. Now I feel empowered and hopeful, but most of all, significant. I can see the valuable ways I contribute to my organization and if I am unclear, I have the confidence to ask how my contributions are being valued. If you want to change how you feel about the work you do or for anything overall, check your belief system. What do you believe about yourself, your role in your company, your value, and the impact of your work? The beliefs you find will be the cookie crumb trail that leads to the emotions you are experiencing.

HOW TO REGULATE YOUR EMOTIONS

Emotional regulation is such an important skill to develop. It helps you avoid taking things personally, keeps you calm in high stressed situations, helps you communicate your needs without damaging relationships, and allows you to remain professional in challenging situations. I will admit, regulating emotions is not an easy task. It takes intentional, daily effort. Every day you must choose to respond versus react. Responding means you consider all sides of a situation as well as the consequences of your actions before you act. Reacting is emotional, immediate, automatic type behavior based on the behavior of someone or a situation. Usually, instant regret follows due to the absence of thinking about the possible consequences of your actions or spoken words. These are ways that work when I need to regulate my emotions.

DISCOVER WHAT CALMS YOU

I find that music and deep breathing exercises are the most effective when I need to calm down. You may find that going for a long walk, journaling, exercise, or another hobby may bring you calm. Take time to discover what works and keep it in mind the next time a situation upsets you. Don't be afraid to ask people who upset you for time to calm down as well. Not every situation needs an immediate response. Often, when emotions are running high, focusing on getting calm should be the top priority.

HONOR YOUR EMOTIONS

When feelings come up, don't wonder why you feel that way. Ask "what" type questions. For example: "What has caused me to feel this way?" "What choices do I have?" "What would make me feel_____ right now?" (fill in the blank with safe, heard, loved, etc.) Taking this approach will validate your emotions and help you avoid the habit of dismissing yourself. You have the right to feel whatever you feel. Explore the feeling and seek to understand it. This is where extending compassion to ourselves as we would to a friend is needed most. Reflecting in this way also provides a learning opportunity to figure out what impacts your emotions. You can use what you learn to educate others in the future on how to interact with you.

CHOOSE HOW TO RESPOND TO YOUR EMOTIONS

Regulating your emotions is requires you to choose how to respond. This doesn't mean you have to suppress your emotions or bottle them up. But it does mean choosing how you will express them in a way that is constructive and helpful, rather than destructive or harmful. Don't be afraid to embrace your emotions – they just might be the key to career success.

MANAGE YOUR STRESS

This is an area I have recently started to address. Failure to do so landed me in the hospital in the beginning of 2022. I highly recommend that you proactively manage your stress by investing in proper nutrition, allowing yourself to get enough rest, engaging in exercise, practicing mindfulness, spending time in the sun (this is my favorite), and spending time with people or pets that love you. Neglecting stress management not only hinders you from being able to regulate your emotions, but it can have dangerous consequences on your health. So please take this seriously and manage your stress. There are three particular behaviors I recommend that you become aware of and eliminate because they are known stressors. These stressor-behaviors are negative thinking, perfectionism, and over-analysis.

I have struggled with these three my entire life, so I want to share some ways you can address these behaviors and eliminate them. First, let's define them. Negative thinking is just like it sounds. It means thinking in a way that views disadvantages, flaws, and why things can't or won't work out. It also means seeing the worst in people, places, and situations. This way of thinking is a recipe for a life of misery. Perfectionism is another negative state of mind as well. It means being in an anxious state of being because you are trying to reach your ideal of perfection, which in most cases is unrealistic. This type of obsessive behavior is often fueled by a fear of being judged, rejected, or criticized. I started and stopped working on the idea for this book for two years because it never felt quite "ready". In actuality, I was delaying the release of something that has the potential to help many people. Lastly, is over-analysis. This means being in a state of constantly dwelling on and analyzing people, situations, and tasks. This can be an excellent trait if performed in moderation. Where it becomes a stressor is when we dwell on and relive situations and mistakes we cannot change or fixate on why people don't do what we think they should do. To counteract these behaviors, you must first become aware of them. Ask a close friend or family member if you display these behaviors. Journal daily and take notice of the times you may display negativity, perfectionism, or over-analysis. Identify what triggered it, ask what caused you to feel that way, and question if it is true. In addition to these recommendations, I suggest taking time to enjoy life. Don't put off taking that vacation or trying that restaurant you have always wanted to go to. Live a little. You'll be surprised by how much tension and stress it will relieve. I treat myself to either a massage, a favorite meal, or trip any time I feel overwhelmed, tired, or stressed. Exercise, laughter, and helping those less fortunate are also great stress relievers to try. Experiment and see what works for you. The other techniques mentioned earlier such as meditation, mindfulness, and discovering what brings you calm also provide an added benefit of reducing stress.

THE CHOICE IS YOURS

The mind is a power tool that can be used for your greatest achievements or your greatest downfall. The path you decide to take is up to you. There is so much more that I can say about the mind and updating our programming because I am so passionate about studying psychology and NeuroLinguistic Programming, yet I am intentionally keeping this book brief because I want you to focus on execution to prepare for your transition into career elevation as soon as possible. It is important to note that this will be a lifelong journey. We are constantly learning, growing, and changing which requires our mindset to be adjusted on a continuous basis. Enjoy the journey. It's a fun ride and you'll love who you will become! Continue to the next chapter so you can discover how to upgrade your skills, which is an essential element to having more career options and fulfillment!

CHAPTER 3:

PERSONAL POWER BEATS PASSIVITY

"Personal Power is the ability to take action."
~ Tony Robbins

Updating your mental programming is just the beginning of upgrading from being passive to powerful. Once you upgrade your mindset, it will be equally important to take intentional action to exercise your personal power. Think of personal power as a muscle. The more you use it, the stronger it becomes. So, what is personal power? As the Tony Robbins quote suggested, it starts with the ability to take action. I would add that it also involves being intentional in the actions you take. If we are committed to leaving the passive life behind, we will need to embrace habits and behaviors that reflect the opposite of being passive which is, confidence, self-awareness, and the ability to connect with others. To reinforce this point, I found an article from BetterUp[1] that defines personal power as an attitude or state of mind where someone is focused on self-efficacy (self-belief), which encompasses all of the things I mentioned above (confidence, self-awareness and people skills). Let's take a deeper dive into what it will take to develop your personal power, starting with being intentional.

BEING INTENTIONAL

It is quite common for us to operate on autopilot when we have a routine that rarely changes. When this is the case, we aren't inspired, excited or looking forward to anything in particular. Being on autopilot can also lead us to overcommit; saying yes to things without considering how the decision will impact us or our lives.

Living intentionally means that you are aware of your actions and why you are doing them. When being intentional, it is important to examine the "why" behind your actions. Your "why" must be something you can immediately refer to when you feel like quitting so you can be inspired you to keep moving forward.

---

[1] What is personal power? Develop your power and own your life. https://www.betterup.com/blog/personal-power.

Here are some suggestions you can use to be intentional.

Plan your day in advance.

I like to write out my daily plan the night before. Like me, you may juggle multiple responsibilities and it can be difficult to balance it all. Using a journal, notebook, or reminders in your smartphone can be a lifesaver. It will help you take control of your day and avoid forgetting things that are important.

Avoid time-consuming and empty activities.

While there is nothing wrong with recreation time, be sure to have it scheduled. Mindlessly scrolling on social or binge watching tv will not help you shift into your personal power and can waste valuable time.

Prioritize your time and self-care.

When you are intentional, you understand that time is much more valuable than money. Time is a limited resource that we cannot get back. Prioritizing our time requires us to focus on the most important things first and continue from there to less important matters. Be choosy in how you spend your time with a conscious awareness of how precious and finite this resource is.

In addition, do not neglect self-care. Our health and wellbeing is a valuable resource that allows us to accomplish the goals and tasks that makes us successful. Be sure to set aside time to do things that will nurture you mental, physical, and spiritual health. This will ensure that you bring the best version of you to the forefront of anything that you do.

SELF-AWARENESS

Pursuing greater self-awareness was a key factor in my transition into a more satisfying career. I define self-awareness as your ability to know who you are and why you do what you do, without criticism or judgment. It also means knowing how you impact those around you and how others impact you. To be self-aware, you must pay attention to yourself, recognize what makes you happy, sad, angry, frustrated, demotivated, etc. You also need to pay attention to how others respond to you.

It is important to increase self-awareness so you can confidently show up in your personal power. The more self-aware I became, the more I realized I would never be valued beyond the level I valued myself. The level you value yourself is based on what you know, appreciate and are able to articulate. As Charles de Lint says – "when you find yourself, everything else follows"; he was absolutely right! Below are the building blocks that helped me increase my self-awareness. No need to rush through these. Take your time and implement each recommendation.

Tune into how you feel

The first step in upgrading your self-awareness is tuning into how you feel about yourself, your career decisions, and your life. Examine your feelings or gut reactions to the following questions: Am I happy? Why or why not?, What do I want? How do I feel about my job right now? Am I satisfied in my current role? Why or why not? What would I choose as a career if I could also choose my salary? In addition to that, you can make notes of how things positively or negatively impact your emotions throughout the day. You can use a spiral notebook, a journal, or a Google doc. By documenting what impacts your feelings, you'll notice patterns. This will help you define what drives, inspires, and motivates you as well as what does the opposite. As a bonus exercise, I highly recommend that you monitor your energy levels throughout the day and take notice of when you have your highest level of energy. This will be the time when you do your best work. Having this information lets you know how to arrange tasks and schedules for the greatest amount of productivity.

Use Assessments

Psychometric assessments have no right or wrong answers, just a set of traits that most accurately describe a person. Gallup Strengthfinders, Myers-Briggs, DISC, and Fascination are the top four I would suggest. They each address different areas and can give you a comprehensive view of yourself. For instance, Strengthfinders identifies the areas where you have the greatest potential for building strength, and measures recurring patterns of thought, feeling, and behavior. Myers-Briggs focuses on identifying your personality type. The DISC assessment focuses on your communication style. The Fascinate Test is the only assessment I've found that identifies your personality archetype based on how others view you.

Taking assessments gave me a better view of myself and opened my eyes to talents and strengths I never considered. This insight gave me clues to the type of work that would motivate me and keep me engaged. It also gave me language that helped me describe my strong attributes and what value they can provide to an organization. While assessments provide a treasure trove of valuable information and insights, it is important to work with a certified professional to help you interpret the results and offer guidance or coaching. I do not recommend simply googling an assessment and making career decisions based on the results. In each of the instances where I took an assessment, it was offered by a company I was affiliated with and was facilitated by a certified professional. Having the results interpreted by a professional was an amazing experience that helped me see the nuances of the results where there were some discrepancies and provided lots of clarity through the discussions. These experiences inspired me to become certified in DISC and Fascinate sciences so I can help clients in the same manner I was helped long ago.

Develop a Habit of Reflection

Having a practice of reflection is the most powerful tool in your self-awareness toolkit. For an hour each night, I review the events of the day. I write in my journal things that were a challenge, things I enjoyed, and areas I can improve. Imagine how much easier life would be if you avoided making the same mistakes. Reflecting on your day and acknowledging your successes and setbacks is an effective way to avoid repeating errors. You can ask yourself questions like, "What could I have done better today?" Based on your answers, you can create a more effective approach for the next time. Be sure to review your successes. We are often too hard on ourselves and do not give ourselves enough credit for the amazing things we do each day. Here are some additional questions you may want to ask yourself during your reflection: What am I trying to accomplish right now? What tasks are helping me achieve my goals? What is slowing down my progress? How can I change the tasks that aren't working so I can achieve my goals?

Create a Career Brag Bank

I created an "all about me folder" early in my career transition. In this folder, I kept detailed notes of what I accomplished in my roles. This folder also included emails that expressed positive or constructive feedback on my performance, evaluations, and other kudos or compliments.

Keeping a record of your accomplishments reinforces your value and provides you proof of your contributions to an organization. It also gives insight on how others view you which often provides a more objective view of yourself since we tend to be more critical of ourselves than others.

Seek feedback regularly from trusted colleagues and friends

Feedback allows us to see our strengths and weaknesses from an objective perspective. Think of it as an honest mirror that provides the reflection you need to see how you perform and how you come across to others. Feedback from trusted co-workers and friends can help us avoid having an inflated and inaccurate perception of our skills and abilities while giving us insights on areas we need to improve. I absolutely love feedback!

Feedback is necessary for our growth and development both personally and professionally, so embrace it. Self-awareness is key to doing your best work. If you do not know who you are, your strengths and weaknesses; you will not be able to make career decisions that are in your best interests. You will find yourself in a holding pattern of going from one unfulfilling position to another: never reaching your full potential nor your income goals. Being self-aware inspires others to have confidence in you. When others have confidence in you, they trust you. People do business with and hire people they trust.

CONFIDENCE

I have found that confidence is built by developing competence. Competence is developed by performing tasks successfully. Performing tasks successfully requires practice and doing tasks that aligns with our strengths. When we are aware of our strengths and weaknesses, we can create a career that aligns with things we do best, and our confidence will then naturally soar. I noticed that whenever I am tasked with things that I am not naturally good at, those are the times I feel the most insecure and self-conscious. This is completely normal, and many people feel this way. To upgrade your confidence, I recommend taking the following actions:

Reflect on your career brag-bank weekly.

This will remind you of your value and strengths, giving you a quick confidence boost. This can be especially helpful in times of uncertainty. Acknowledging your successes will also increase the chances of those things being repeated.

Embrace failure.

This may not sound like a way to boost your confidence, but it actually works. Embracing failures allows you to view them as learning experiences. It is through our failures that we develop the strength and perseverance necessary to achieve our goals. When we face our fears and embrace our failures, we open the door to new opportunities for growth and success. Failure teaches you more about yourself and shows you what you are capable of. If you are willing to face your failures head-on, they can be the key to unlocking your potential and amplifying your confidence.

Present yourself with confidence.

How we feel about yourself is reflected in our appearance. Your presentation is much more than wearing trendy clothes. Instead, it's all about being poised, feeling self-assured and having a confident posture in any situation. This can include posture, gestures, facial expressions, and eye movement. How you carry yourself speaks volumes about your confidence level. Try practicing facial expressions, postures, and power poses in the mirror, if you're unsure about what power poses are, do a quick google search. Upgrading your wardrobe is still helpful to ensure that you present yourself in the best light. We'll talk more about this in the chapter on personal branding.

PEOPLE SKILLS

People skills boil down to two things in my opinion; communication and your ability to interact with people well. "Having good people skills means maximizing effective and productive human interaction to everyone's benefit", says Lynn Taylor[2], a national workplace expert and author of "Tame Your Terrible Office Tyrant; How to Manage Childish

---

[2] 20 People Skills You need to Succeed at Work https://www.forbes.com/sites/jacquelynsmith/2013/11/15/the-20-people-skills-you-need-to-succeed-at-work/

Boss Behavior and Thrive in Your Job". I most definitely agree with this. When it comes to human interaction, communication reigns supreme. Communication includes conveying your thoughts and ideas clearly and respectfully as well as listening intently. Listening is one of my superpowers. I am attentive to not only what is said, but also what is not said, tone, body language, eye contact, etc. Listening is a skill definitely worth cultivating if you want to interact well with others.

On the other hand, interacting with others requires you to be intentional on being likable[3] and relatable. Ways that you can be likable is to listen well, be supportive, look for commonalities and try not to overtalk others. To be relatable, what I have found to work for me is to simply be genuine. We as human beings all have an inner B.S. detector and can instantly tell when someone is not being real or authentic. So, just be yourself in a way that is appropriate to the setting you're in. Focusing on others will also help you become relatable. I teach my children to be "others conscious" which simply means to be aware of how you can be helpful to others and avoid solely focusing on yourself when interacting with others.

Now, it is common knowledge that not everyone will get along because some personalities do not mesh, however, we can use skills such as courtesy, curiosity, empathy, and kindness to smooth those interactions over. I believe we all

---

[3] https://www.psychologytoday.com/us/blog/the-squeaky-wheel/202009/10-ways-become-more-likable

should carry ourselves in a professional manner and treat people as we would like to be treated. There are times that this is difficult, and we come across personalities that are more challenging to deal with than others. This is when I would recommend a book called "How to cope with difficult people" by Alain Houel and Christian Godefroy. I listened to the audio version of this book every day when I was working in a role that had me dealing with several difficult subject matter experts and team leaders. The great thing about this book is that it also offers talking points and strategies to use.

You now know that the key to developing your personal power is to be intentional daily, upgrade your self-awareness, boost your confidence, and refine your people skills. Embracing your personal power will beat passivity every time! That's exactly what you want if you are going to shift from passive to powerful in your career! The next step in the UPGRADE Method is to get a power circle which is what you'll explore in the next chapter, so keep reading.

CHAPTER 4:

GET A POWER CIRCLE

You're The Average Of The Five People You Spend The Most Time With ~ Jim Rohn

Relationships are the most valuable asset you can have in your career. Having the right relationships can open doors to opportunities, provide support, and offer valuable insights as you grow and develop. Until now, you may not have proactively chosen the people you are around most. Perhaps you have childhood friends, family members, or old co-workers that you connect with based on familiarity or circumstances. Some may think they are strong enough to be around anyone while still reaching their goals, even if they are negative. This is a huge misconception. Human nature cannot be denied. We reflect and adopt attributes from our environment. So, if you are truly determined to shift from passive to powerful so you can turn career frustration to career elevation, you must be strategic about your relationships and intentionally choose who you spend the most time with.

Everyone needs a Power Circle, which is in essence the top five to six people you spend most of your time with. These individuals each have specific roles to play in order to ensure you develop into your best self. Let's look at each.

SIX ROLES IN THE POWER CIRCLE

The Sage

This person serves as a source of wisdom. I've always enjoyed being in the company of my elders. The stories, insights, and guidance are always priceless. These individuals can see further than you because of their experience and can spare you the pain of learning by mistakes. Keep in mind that a sage can also be someone who is younger than you. Wisdom is applied knowledge and experience, so it is likely that you may come across someone who has the wisdom you need but is younger than you. Don't miss those opportunities by overlooking someone based on their age. You'll be surprised what you may learn. So always have a sage or two in your circle!

The Lighthouse

This person provides guidance (light) when you are down or in the thick of your challenges. They help you see your way through. They may not be as wise as the sage, but they know what you're going through and how to get out of it. They remind you of what you have inside and check to make sure you keep meet your goals. My therapist, sister, mentor, and other elders at different periods of my life have been lighthouses. The nice thing is that you can have different people at different times. No matter what, you need a lighthouse in your circle for sure!

The Firestarter

This person serves as your motivator, coach, or cheerleader! They get you "fired up" and don't mind calling you out for procrastination or slacking. They may ask you, "How bad do you want this?" to challenge your resolve to be who you said you wanted to be. They'll remind you of the vision you have and charge you to keep going after it. We cannot achieve greatness without having someone in our lives who is willing to put a bit of fire under our butts! My best friend and sisters have always been the fire in my life. Sometimes what they say makes me mad, yet I can't deny the truth of their words, especially when it comes to fulfilling my purpose. If you don't have a Firestarter in your circle, start looking now!

The Visionary

This person sees more in you than you see in yourself. They are confident in your abilities, and you may need to borrow their confidence at times to take action towards your goals. Visionaries are also great at selling us on the possibilities. They may see gifts in you that you aren't utilizing and inspire you to look again and try something new. Although we must work on believing in ourselves, we also need to have those around us who believe, too. Find your visionary and ensure they're in your circle. I have a few visionaries in my circle. My best friend, colleagues, and my business coach always provide insights on my blind spots when it comes to my potential. These are invaluable people you must have in your life!

The Thinking Partner

This person may be in the same field or a similar field as you. You can brainstorm, problem-solve, and generate ideas with a thinking partner. One of my thinking partner is one of my sisters. We both study psychology and are fascinated with human nature, yet we focus on different aspects of it. Our conversations are two hours or more and they always generate ideas, aha-moments, and insights we couldn't get on our own. My co-workers and one of my mentors are also amazing thinking partners. You need a thinking partner for career moves, changes, challenges, or simply to talk through things. Be sure it's reciprocal and be sure to have more than one. This is where joining a mastermind group can be invaluable!

The Connector

This person will be able to connect you to other people, resources, or opportunities based on their perception of your value and the mutually beneficial nature of your relationship. I've had the pleasure of adding a few new connectors in my power circle through my podcast, *Embrace the Upgrade*. I also have connectors on my job and from connections I made on LinkedIn.

I've found these key roles to be essential in my career, and I believe they will be essential in yours as well. Keep in mind that one person may fulfill multiple roles. That's ok. My sister is my thinking partner and lighthouse at times. My best friend is the Firestarter and Visionary. The key is to become familiar with the descriptions and seek out individuals who can fill those roles. It is also important for you to fill these roles in the lives of others. I've discovered that based on my strengths and experiences, my primary role in other people's lives is the sage, visionary, and thinking partner. For my children, I'm all of these. The nature of the relationship and your strengths will inform you of the role you need to play. So, pay attention. Be ready to serve where needed.

BUILD YOUR POWER CIRCLE THROUGH POWER NETWORKING

Knowing the proper way to network is crucial for building your power circle or any relationship. Power networking, as I call it, is a life skill and a lifestyle. It involves meeting people and building relationships in a systematic way to build a mutually beneficial and profitable professional network. It is also important because you want to surround yourself with likeminded people because as Jim Rohn's quotes suggests, who we are around affects who we become. So, if you are truly determined to shift from career frustration to career elevation, you must surround yourself with people who are on the same journey, or who are already where you want to be. Power Networking is the key to getting you there. Keep in mind, this is not an activity you do only when you want something. It's an ongoing process that creates long-term, mutually beneficial relationships. Given that I have seen networking done wrong more often than not, let's discuss what networking looks like when done properly.

Networking done right is based on two fundamental concepts – abundance and reciprocity. Abundance means you operate from a belief that there is plenty of everything to go around. This requires an abundance mindset. When you can live into this way of thinking, you do not feel the need to compete. Rather, you are eager to contribute and collaborate. If you struggle with an abundance mindset, I have an abundance journal[4] with prompts that can help you develop this way of thinking.

The second concept is reciprocity, which is a fancy word for the simple concept of when you do something good for others, it comes back to you multiplied. If you help others with no expectations, their natural response will be to help you in return. This is the 'power' of power networking. The key is keeping the idea that you are a resource for others in the forefront of your mind. Of course, you want some benefits from building your network, but this shouldn't be your main focus. Instead, you are a resource who others in your network can count on. When you pay it forward in this way, helping others solve their problems with your knowledge and expertise, they'll be inclined to help you.

---

[4] https://shannondsmith.com/shop/

Keep in mind that long before you expect anything out of the people you meet, you need to get to know them. There is no short-term gain in power networking. Everything is done for the long-term benefits. First, you build trust, rapport, and effective communication with the contacts you meet. It takes time to earn trust and build rapport, so you don't start asking for favors immediately. It is essential to use this skill regularly, and before you need anything. Because the central idea behind power networking is paying it forward by offering to help others, you need to be clear on your unique value or abilities. A number of skills are needed to network effectively. There are six core skills that I work with clients on developing when coaching them one-on-one. Here is a condensed version of the core skills you need:

Ability to approach others – How hard is it for you to strike up a conversation with strangers or introduce yourself?

Non-verbal communication skills – How well does your posture and facial expressions match what you're saying verbally?

Conversation skills – Do you know when to interject, how to maintain a balance between talking and listening, and keep a conversation going?

Listening – You need to pay attention to what others say to help you find commonalities.

Confidence – You must be able to communicate to others the expertise, knowledge, skills, and other benefits you offer them.

Positivity – A big smile, plenty of enthusiasm, and a positive feeling that inspires others.

THE POWER NETWORKING PROCESS

The Power Networking Process, which I teach in my coaching program, is fully loaded so I won't include everything in this chapter, but I will give you the framework and essentials to put into action so you can set yourself up for success when networking. The steps below will help you maximize your networking and ensure that the connections you make are mutually valuable as you progress towards career elevation.

Research – This is where you do your groundwork in finding the people you want to network with. You're going to be looking for people who can help you meet your goals.

Connect – This is where you will leverage a variety of ways to connect with the people you identified in your research.

Follow-Up – Following up is a critical part of networking and is key to building lasting relationships.

Outcome – At this point of the process you look at the results of your follow-up to decide on next steps.

Measure – You need to frequently measure the results of your networking to see if you're achieving your goals.

Refine – As with any planning, you should continually refine your action plans after checking in on results.

POWER NETWORKING BEST PRACTICES

A good place to start is by identifying people who are currently in your network. Even if you have never intentionally networked, you know many people who can help you. Once you start writing down names, you may be surprised. For each person, write down how you know them, what they've done for you in the past, what you've done for them in the past, and how you'll continue to interact with them. The last element is where you'll need to be creative. After you've made your list, reach out to them, and let them know about your career goal and what you are trying to achieve. Ask if they know of anyone you should meet or talk to. If they do, also ask if they would be willing to introduce you. Having them introduce you allows you to borrow their credibility with the new contact.

Craft Your Story. How you present yourself to others is important in power networking. A major part of this is your 'story.' This is the story you tell about yourself when you meet new people, and it contains everything you need them to know about you. What you're doing is condensing the usual 'get to know you' conversation so it's quick and easy for other people to understand in a short amount of time. Keep in mind that an introductory story isn't all you need. This is just the beginning. You'll need a fuller, more detailed version of your story to tell people as you get deeper into conversation. You also need questions to ask to get to know the other person. After drafting your initial story, create several variations for different situations. You may create alternate versions for distinct types of people you meet or different goals that you have in your networking. As you network, you'll also learn how to improvise and alter your story to match the situation.

Evaluate your networking skills. Before you attend a networking function, realistically evaluate the skills you have and the skills you need. Through this evaluation, you can create a roadmap that will help guide your networking efforts. Think about your own networking skills and the skills you need to acquire to attain your goals. Also, consider what you can offer to people you meet. What unique abilities can you provide? How do you help others in your work or daily life? How have you helped others in the past? What are your most outstanding achievements? These will reveal potentially valuable contributions you can offer your network.

Build connections that matter. Connect with people who can add value to your career goals, expand your professional reach, and increase your visibility. When starting out, it can be difficult to know who you should reach out to and how to get started. These tips can help steer you in the right direction.

Start by interacting with people in your chosen field of business.

When I decided to change careers from customer service to instructional design, I reached out to instructional designers at my job. Then I expanded my networking to LinkedIn and other trade/industry associations. Look for educators, department heads, industry leaders, decision-makers, and role models who work in your chosen industry. Follow colleagues in your industry and move in similar circles that will help you build connections.

Engage and interact with people by sharing their work and commenting on their posts or articles.

In essence, be social on social. Mingle, keep yourself relevant, and engage with those who engage with you. If anyone outside your network engages with you, send them a request to connect. Check out their professional profile and see if it aligns with your career and business objectives. Be true to your brand. Connect with people who align with your values, mission, and goals. Make sure you are consistent when building your network. Keep the conversations going, keep connecting, and keep engaging.

Engaging regularly makes you more recognizable and visible to the people and organizations you want to attract, and it will keep you abreast of industry developments and openings. Also, remember the importance of adding value. No one wants to be bombarded with requests from someone they do not know. When engaging online, leave comments that add value, inspiration, or perspective. Find and send resources to your connections that you think they would appreciate. Let them know you were thinking of them and thought the resource would be helpful. Offer your expertise, skills, or talents in some significant way. Be creative! When you reach out to connect with someone, be sure to emphasize the benefits they will receive by being in your network. Think about how you will create a mutually beneficial relationship with the people you want to connect with before you reach out.

YOU'LL GET BETTER WITH PRACTICE

When you first start networking, remember that it's perfectly all right to be nervous. Everyone is, even though they may not show it. As you network more consistently, it gets easier because you have more experience and can improve your strategy and methods over time. Eventually, every step in the process, from finding events to following up, will become second nature and you will be a Power Networking Pro!

Now that you know what it takes to build your power circle and how to use power networking to do it, I want to shift gears to help you use all you've learned so far to relaunch your personal brand. To be prepared for your transition into career elevation, you must be visible and known for something. So, keep reading to find out how. I'm so excited about what's in store for you in the next chapter!

CHAPTER 5:

REVAMP YOUR PERSONAL BRAND

Brand yourself for the career you want, not the job you have. ~ Dan Schawbel

No matter what career path you're on, you are in marketing and sales first. I know it may be hard for you to agree with that statement, but just go with me for a moment. Before you landed your current job, you had to highlight the skills, experience, and education that would be of interest to the employer you were targeting. You created marketing materials (resume, cover letters, LinkedIn) with these skills, experiences, and education on them to attract interest (in essence, these are your features and benefits). If someone became interested in what you had to offer, they would reach out and schedule a meeting to learn more. During the sales call (phone screen), you had to sell the potential client (recruiter) on you being the only logical choice for what they were looking for. If the call went well, you would be invited to another meeting (interview) where you had to make a sales presentation and sell the idea of purchasing a bulk amount of your time (product) at an annual rate (salary) in exchange for a specific set of outcomes (services) that your employer (client) desired. If you did a decent job selling them on your value, you would sign a contract (new hire paperwork) to seal the deal. In most cases, you would get a percentage of your annual rate at an agreed upon frequency and additional bonuses may be an option based on performance. So, you see, your first objective is to market yourself before you ever do your actual job.

Now that we've established that marketing and sales come first, let's look at the steps to build your personal brand with intention.

WHY HAVING A PERSONAL BRAND IS IMPORTANT

Your personal brand helps differentiate you from others by showing what is unique about you. People remember you before they remember what you do. No matter what your particular goal is, your personal brand has a huge impact on whether or not people want to work with you, Developing a strong personal brand brings huge advantages to your career or business such as being seen as the 'go-to person in your industry.

BUILDING A PERSONAL BRAND

Dan Schawbel says, "Brand yourself for the career you want, not the job you have." From now on, I want you to take ownership of your career by crafting a personal brand based on where you want to go versus where you are now. Your compensation is directly tied to your perceived value and the results you produce. To perform at a high level, you must do work that aligns with who you are and what you can do well, which is why the self-discovery process must be completed before working on your personal brand.

Personal branding is for everyone, not just businesses and entrepreneurs. When you think about some of the biggest and most successful brands today, you also think about the people behind them. Naturally, the feelings and impressions you have about those entrepreneurs influences your perception of their work. We no longer have the luxury of anonymity. We are all online. However, intentionally developing a personal brand is a way of controlling the narrative about who you are and what you stand for. Oprah is a perfect example of someone who does this extremely well! If you pay attention to her example, there are many lessons to be learned. It would take too long to go into all of them, but I will say, she decides what projects she is involved in based on whether they align with what she stands for, or her objectives. She is selective in who she interviews and associates with and she chooses movie roles that are congruent with who she is. We can do the same in our career.

Being intentional in our personal branding is being selective with our affiliations, published content, accepted roles, and projects we participate in. It is also key to removing the barrier that exists between you and your next opportunity. Personal branding is the way you present yourself to your ideal audience, whether that is a company, or individuals.

GET CLEAR ON THE VISION FOR YOUR BRAND

When you create a personal brand, you begin by clarifying your personal vision. Being clear about your vision means you know the path you're following, which makes it easier to set goals. You can't control every aspect of your life, but you can create a long-term vision and set goals to achieve that vision. After all, only you can determine how you want your life to unfold. Focus on the vison you have for your life as a whole, not just your career, so that you can identify what's important for you to achieve. If you haven't defined your personal vision before, don't feel overwhelmed. There are practical tools that can help, such as a vision board. Here are some examples of vision boards:

If you prefer to create your vision board online, there are wide varieties of software programs and free apps available, including Canva[5] or Pinterest[6]. A tangible, handmade one keeps your focus for longer and creates better connections to your subconscious mind. Some people use both methods depending on their goals.

Define Your Values

Your values are the foundation of your personal brand, so you need to know what they are. Values are basic human principles that guide our lives. We know them to be true for us, even if others may have different values. Values are important because they help us behave consistently in all situations and make difficult decisions. Examples of values are dependability, integrity, well-being and sustainability.

Find Out How Others See You

Defining your positive qualities and core values is an important step to building your personal brand. Other people may see things in you that you haven't noticed, or you take for granted. So, consulting with others can help you get to know yourself better. Talk to people you trust and who know you well. Ask them what they think of you. Your close friends, a mentor, or a coach are good options. You can also ask a trusted manager, client or co-worker who knows you well and with whom you've worked for a long time if you feel comfortable. They can tell you why they enjoy working with you and what they value in you. If you're tempted to ask your family, only choose family members you can count on to be constructive. Compare what you learned about yourself with what other people said.

Decide What You Want to Be Known For

Your brand is also about what you want to be known for in your field. People with strong personal brands are noticed because they share their passion for what they do. This passion comes from within and is often connected to their strengths and expertise. When you get clear about the expertise you have and how you want to use it, you'll find what you want to be known for and share this passion with your audience. For example, do you want to be the go-to person in your industry for something specific? Choose your key areas of expertise, the ones that help you stand out. This will help when you identify who you want to work with.

Choose Who You Want to Work With

Having a personal brand is not just about you. Your branding is also about the people who receive your message. Anyone who looks you up, such as a potential business partner or a prospective employer, will see your branding. When you know your audience well, you'll know what information is appropriate to share. You'll know what things you have in common and what experiences you share.

Your Personal Brand Message

Your brand message will clarify your unique value, which is what makes you different and attracts certain people to work with you. It's your chance to position yourself in the marketplace. Start by describing your unique value you in a few words. This needs one or two sentences that say succinctly what you do and what benefits you bring. Here's an idea of a template you can use:

"I help XX people who want XXX to XXX because I have the XXX experience/skills they need"

For example: I help recruitment consultants who want to double their revenue to motivate their team to find more clients because of my 25 years successfully running a recruitment agency.

Then clarify what it is that makes people want to work with you. Refer back to the previous module for this information if you need to. You may also have received comments on this from past customers.

For example: My clients really appreciate the fact that I support and motivate them through their journey until they achieve their goals.

You can then add something about you personally as this is your personal brand.

For example: When I'm not working, I relax with a good book, or I love cats and have four of them. Put this together to create your personal brand message. Review what you've written and cut unnecessary words or phrases that don't specifically explain the benefits of working with you.

Use Career-Focused Digital Marketing

Essentially, career-focused digital marketing is using digital platforms and strategies to market yourself to people and organizations within your chosen career. When organizations launch a new product, they undertake a marketing campaign to determine what promotional activities they need to do, where their target audience is, and how much they want the product. Think of your job search as a career marketing campaign, with yourself as the product. You will then package your knowledge, skills, and experience in a way that will attract buyers of your services. Your campaign may include content published on LinkedIn or a blog, your resume, a personal website, and any other online profiles. A more advanced strategy is to target specific companies and launch an outreach campaign where you will proactively reach out to points of contact at organizations to see if they have an opening based on your criteria and what you have to offer. If you are looking for your next job, an employer would be the buyer and your services are the results you can secure using your knowledge, skills, and experience.

When coaching clients one-on-one, I walk through this process step-by-step to create their career-focused digital marketing campaign which includes all elements of personal branding so they can attract the opportunities they desire.

Managing Your Online Presence and Reputation

Online reputation management refers to building, improving, or restoring your name on the Internet. Before you read any further, try this little experiment: Google your name, in quotes, and see what comes up. Take a look at the results. Is there anything that makes you feel uncomfortable? Do you feel okay with what people will see at the top of the list? Scroll down. Do you like what content shows up further down the page? When people hear or see your name, they should automatically think of the problem solve or the solution you provide. Proactive online reputation management means taking control of your reputation online by employing various strategies that are both proactive and reactive (if damage control is needed). I have a full course on this topic, but I'll provide the brief version here. Online reputation management, also called ORM, is more than just social media monitoring, but it isn't a full PR campaign. It involves simple tools and techniques that anyone can use. There are five steps and three essential strategies for building and maintaining a good reputation online.

Here are the essential steps:

Step 1 – Assess your current reputation – Gain an understanding of how people see you.

Step 2 - Identify changes needed – Evaluate the results you found from your search and determine what adjustments should be made.

Step 3 - Determine your best arenas – On what platform(s) are people talking about you most? Focus your communication there.

Step 4 - Create a reputation management strategy – This includes what type of content will work best, where to publish it, and how to respond to both positive and negative comments.

Step 5 - Start building - start creating and publishing your content. You will discover what works and what doesn't through trial and error.

Essential Strategies for building and maintaining your online reputation

Post the Right Content Regularly

You can balance out content about you from others by consistently posting your own official content. Post relevant content in the right places online and maintain the integrity of your message.

Keep Private Information Private

Decide what personal information is okay to make public and what information isn't. Keep an eye on your information. Manage your privacy settings on social media sites to carefully control who can see what content.

Deal Quickly with Negative Comments and Publicity

When negative content is posted about you, deal with it as quickly as possible before too many people see it. Deal with it in an appropriate way, keeping in mind that others will see your response. Always respond with your best customer service possible, and never reply with more negativity.

Create a reputation strategy that encompasses your target companies or clients, along with a structure for creating relevant content that speaks to them directly. Implement these steps and strategies for maintaining control over key areas of your online reputation.

CRAFTING YOUR MARKETING MATERIALS

A great way to build your brand online is to craft your materials. Marketing materials include your resume, cover letters, social media profiles, personal websites, blogs, etc. You can build your credibility through the content you share on these platforms and demonstrate to potential employers that you are knowledgeable and relatable. Anything you use to market yourself, whether that is online or not, should be professional and relevant to the opportunities you are seeking.

Relaunching your personal brand requires a mixture of managing how you present yourself and how others see you. It is important to be aware of them both to be successful. Remember, your personal brand is a reflection of you. Don't be afraid to be authentic. But do so authentically. In our society, we often have a misconception that to be vulnerable and authentic requires us share all aspects of our life. This is not true. In fact, it can be repelling to overshare. Think about how you would conduct yourself in a face-to-face interaction. Would you just walk up to someone and share your life story? Of course not, so be strategic in how you show up online, valuing quality over quantity.

Your personal brand also requires you to be consistent and accountable to those you seek to serve. Just like you show up to work daily and on time, show up for your brand in the same manner. Some strategies for growing your personal brand and authority may include creating content in the form of videos, blog posts, or social media posts. Another way to amplify your personal brand is to reach out to people in your industry. Befriending successful people will have you appear successful by association. To do this effectively, refer back to the networking portion in the Revamp Your Power Circle of chapter. Additionally, be sure to have a polished appearance. This is the best way to live out your personal brand. Remember, you are the physical expression of your personal brand, so make sure you have a look that matches it. Dressing well shows that you are a professional and take pride in your brand.

The last element of your personal brand that I want to cover is sharing your story. Throughout this book I have shared various parts of my story as it relates to helping you shift from passive to powerful so you can take control of your career. You can do the same. Sharing your story helps people get a sense of familiarity with you and allows them to see your human side. You should share stories like what led you to choose your career, why you are passionate about what you do, and what challenges you had to overcome. These stories add a level of authenticity and can help build a strong connection between you and your audience. Stories are especially great to tell during interviews. I recommend creating a story bank that you can reference. You can use your catalog of stories anywhere, such as the about me page on your website, social media, when you are a guest on a podcast, or for speaking engagements. Remember, there is a such thing as oversharing, so be mindful of that when crafting your stories. Keep them professional, concise, and impactful. Keep in mind how you want people to feel when hearing the story, and what you want them to do afterwards. This will guide you in what to include and exclude.

Effective personal branding elevates your presence. According to Google, most employers research potential candidates by conducting online searches. This means that your online presence is more important than ever. After all, we all know that first impressions count. Make sure the first time any potential client or employer 'sees' your online profile, it is the best possible version of yourself. Your online branding will reinforce what you offer and set you apart from the competition. Carrying aspects of your branding with you in your everyday life will create authority in your work. It shows that you are serious and credible—that your vision for yourself is a reality. Living your brand is the best way to accomplish this. Now that you know what it will take to relaunch your personal brand, let's consider what it will take to plan for your shift from career frustration to career elevation.

CHAPTER 6:

AMPLIFY YOUR SKILL SET

"The future belongs to those who learn more skills and combine them in creative ways."
– Robert Greene

Can you say with confidence the skills you have today will enable you to maintain and continually improve your quality of life? If your answer is no, it's time to focus on skill building. In order to achieve career success, it's important to focus on amplifying your skills. This means dedicating time and energy to learning new skills and updating your existing ones. Our skills have an expiration date and it's shorter than you think. Research says that skills typically last no more than five years and technical skills last no more than two years due to skill obsolescence, which is when professionals lack the current knowledge or skills necessary to maintain effective performance in their current or future positions. It is also reflected in a change in the skills needed within an occupation, industry, or organization.

As today's workforce continues to change, we need to get comfortable with proactively learning new skills and adapting. Effective skill development can reduce underemployment, increase your marketability, and improve your quality of living. If you are resistant to change, you will put yourself in a vulnerable position where you will be left behind and unable to compete in the workforce. This will look like being made redundant, demoted, or having minimal ability to earn what you need. Upskilling is no longer an option; it is a necessity. I can't stress that enough. Skill development was essential in my career transformation. During the later phase of me working in call-center customer service, I stumbled upon Instructional Design as a career path. I quickly realized that I didn't know what it would take to become an Instructional Designer. I decided to look up Instructional Designers at my call-center. I shared with each of them that I was considering Instructional Design as a career path and asked if they would be open to a fifteen-minute interview. I didn't know it then, but this is called an informational interview. Surprisingly, they all said yes. So, for about a month I conducted interviews on my lunch break. I'd ask questions about what a typical day was like, what skills and education were needed and how they became an Instructional Designer. Each person had a different story and recommendations. This was encouraging to me because it meant that I could possibly forge my own path. In the evening, I'd review my notes and look for skills that all the Instructional Designers had in common. Then I created a plan which outlined the transferable skills I had that would fit into this new career. In the second part of my plan, I listed the skills I didn't have and how I intended to close the skill gaps. While learning and preparing for a career change, I took advantage of learning opportunities such as courses, webinars, and virtual internships. By doing these things, I began to get better job offers as time went on.

Don't make the mistake of overlooking your transferable skills. They are critical for securing roles in new careers and industries. Transferrable skills are skills that can be useful in a variety of roles in different industries. For instance, my ability to change careers from call-center customer service to instructional design was made possible because of my communication skills, technical proficiency, ability to build rapport, problem solving skills and the ability to learn quickly. Having those transferable skills allowed me to qualify for an internship which helped me gain the experience I needed to land my first paid position as an instructional designer. So, don't discount any of your skills. You never know which ones will be the key that unlocks your next opportunity.

As a HR Certified Trainer and Certified Career Coach, I'm very passionate about helping professionals improve their skills. One thing you must know is there's little growth in jobs that require minimal skills or education. They are quickly being absorbed into other positions or replaced by technology. More than 40 million people lost their jobs or were furloughed since the beginning of the COVID-19 pandemic in 2020. While in many cases layoffs were unavoidable, innumerable people remained gainfully employed and continued to thrive. This was largely due to the skills these individuals possessed that were considered essential. I believe that by developing essential, in-demand skills, you can make yourself indispensable, and future-proof your career. The key is to take proactive, intentional action to make it happen!

Developing competence in any skill takes time, dedication, and hard work. Amplifying your skills is important because it allows you to not only become an expert in your field, but it also positions you to contribute to the further development of your craft. Making meaningful contributions makes you stand out and increases your ability to make more money.

Many of us have heard that it takes 10,000 hours of practice to reach mastery level in a skill. This concept originated from research conducted by Dr. K. Anders Erikson of Florida State University. The focus of the study was on high performance individuals such as athletes, singers, chess players, and musicians. So, the 10,000-hour law applies to individuals who want to achieve expert level performance in highly competitive fields. It's safe to say that most of us do not fall in this category. This is good news, because it means there is hope for us to achieve a proficient level of mastery in our chosen career and still experience fulfillment and success. If I had to recommend one book on mastery, it would be Robert Greene's book called Mastery. This is a phenomenal book that shares stories of historical figures who have reached the heights of mastery in their fields while also outlining practical ways we can achieve mastery in our work. In the meantime, I want to give you some practical guidance on how to develop proficiency in any skill. I caution you to choose your skills wisely. Select skills that align with your values and natural talents. By doing so, you will increase your career satisfaction. I recommend choosing skills that can be integrated with skills you already have.

BEST PRACTICES FOR SKILL BUILDING

Select and Break Down the Skill

Choose skills you have enough interest in, so you don't mind devoting the necessary time for focused practice. Notice I said practice. To learn skills effectively, you must assimilate enough information to take some form of action. After taking action to implement what you learn, you'll discover what you retained and what you need to review. Passively watching online courses will not build your skills. Doing do will cause you to have an illusion of competence. Then, when you attempt to use the skill, you'll quickly discover what you don't know.

Once you have selected your skill(s), break them down into smaller sub-skills. Most skills are made up smaller skills. Let's look at the skill of speaking, for example. Within the skill of speaking are several micro skills such as pronunciation, tone, projection, vocabulary, inflection, etc. So, when you look at the skill you are intending to develop, make a list of all the smaller, micro skills that make up the skill you have selected. This will ease some of the overwhelm you may feel when initially deciding to learn a new skill. Work on the subskill you feel most comfortable with and start structuring your learning sessions.

Structure Your Learning Sessions

Your learning sessions should consist of the right tools, environment, and uninterrupted time to learn your new skill. The right tools are dependent upon the skill you are learning. For example, if you are learning computer programming, you would need a computer and the appropriate software to learn to code. Your environment should be learning-friendly, meaning no clutter, well-lit, with natural light if possible, and free of any distractions. It also important to schedule dedicated time to focus on learning and then dedicated time to practice the skill. Try to make sure your learning sessions are around the same day and time since our brains like routines. This will minimize some (not all) of the resistance you'll experience while learning something new. To learn more about overcoming resistance, I highly recommend reading, The War of Art. It will change your life!

Implement a Learning Strategy

The idea of a learning strategy was something foreign to me until I began working on my master's degree in Instructional Design. It was at this point in my life that I discovered we were never taught how to learn in school. Instead, we were told what to learn. We were conditioned to memorize answers, not think critically, research, and challenge ideas. Unfortunately, many never learn how to learn. Given that you have read this far, it won't be you. I'm going to give you some principles on how to learn so you can use them in your learning strategy. This will not be a fully comprehensive list of suggestions, but you will have enough to get started and see great progress.

Space out your learning time - This is known as distributed practice. I like the pomodoro method where you can focus intently for 20 minutes and then take a break. Rest is a must in learning. It gives the brain a chance to process what you've learned. You can study and rehearse for up to 90 minute per day, but that would be the max. This method improves the likelihood of you remembering and retaining what you learn as opposed to cramming for 5+ hours.

Teach what you have learned -While in graduate school, I used my children as students (most of the time unwillingly) to test my level of understanding. If I could get my 9-year-old at the time to understand the stages of learning, then I knew I had grasped the concept. Try teaching what you learn to identify areas you need to focus on and keep repeating it until you can teach with ease. You can also try to explain aloud your thought process and your understanding of what you're learning by asking yourself questions.

Elaboration - Come up with meaningful examples of your own that relate to the skill you are learning. The more you can relate your examples to the new concepts you are learning, the faster you'll learn the new information.

Test your knowledge - The fancy terminology for this is retrieval practice, but you get the gist. In essence, you are going to force yourself to remember information by asking yourself questions or taking practice tests. LinkedIn Learning is great about this; however, you can always create your own study questions or leverage the questions from whatever materials you are using. The more you force recall, the deeper the information goes into your memory.

Get practical experience - Putting new knowledge and skills into practice is one of the best ways to learn. As I mentioned earlier, you want to take in enough information to take action. What you will learn as you take action will be more valuable to you than what you read in a book or learn in an online course. The reason for this is because you are fully immersed in practicing the skill. Think about learning a foreign language. You'll be more successful if you learn in the country of that language and be forced to remember vocabulary and speak the language than if you simply read a book or take an online course. One way to do this is to seek out stretch assignments at your current job, volunteer at another organization, or create projects of your own to apply your new skills.

Avoid Multitasking - For a long time, multi-taking was an admirable trait. Now, research tells us that multi-tasking actually harms our brains and can make learning less effective because it negatively impacts attention and comprehension.

So, from now on, start focusing your attention on one task at a time and decide how much time you will dedicate to learning.

Like anything else, developing competence in any skill will require practice. The more you perform a task, the better you'll become at it. Embrace mistakes. As much as the perfectionist in me hates to say this, making mistakes is part of the learning process. Embrace them and use them as an opportunity to learn and grow. To reach mastery, you need to be constantly learning and growing as a professional. This means reading books, taking courses, and attending workshops. It also means being open to innovative ideas and ways of doing things. Be patient with yourself and don't get discouraged if you don't see results immediately. Just keep working hard and you will reach your goals!

WHAT ABOUT PASSIONS?

Your passions are important, but not most important in my opinion. While passion will be a factor in your career, the need for specific skill sets that solve pressing problems is what leads to a sustainable career. Keep in mind that an organization hires because they're looking for someone who has the skills to solve a problem for them. The same is true for being a freelancer or entrepreneur. Clients look for businesses who are able to solve a problem for them. You must have in-demand skills that solve pressing problems. As you apply these skills and successfully solve problems for clients or your organization, your passion will surface and grow because you're contributing in a meaningful way. A book I highly recommend in this area is titled, So Good They Can't Ignore You by Cal Newport. This book changed my perspective in my career journey and helped me shift my focus from an emphasis on looking for what I enjoy doing to discovering what I am naturally talented at that can develop into a marketable skillset. My discovery led to a lucrative career and ultimately, fulfillment.

Remember, it's not just about doing your job well.

Now that you know why it's important to prioritize skill building and how to develop an effective learning strategy, I want to help you position yourself more powerfully at work. When it comes to skill building, you cannot focus solely on your technical aptitude and expect to be successful. When I say technical, I don't simply mean computer skills or the ability to use various applications. Technical skills are also specialized knowledge like project management, instructional design, product management, etc. While these skills are important, they pale in comparison to what your primary focus should be. If you want people to value you, you must develop beyond just doing your job well. You will need to develop four essential soft skills.

According to the Carnegie Institute of Technology, 85 percent of our financial success is due to personality and the ability to communicate, negotiate, and lead. It's amazing to me that only 15 percent of our financial success is a result of technical knowledge. For years, I had it backwards. It wasn't until about 2017 that things clicked for me. I was working as a government contractor at the time, and I connected instantly with one of my supervisors. I noticed how she was able to communicate with anyone in the organization and had a way of making people feel seen and heard. Everyone seemed to like her, and everyone knew her. I learned of her quick rise to her position and was simply amazed! She had less technical ability than me and often sought my advice on how to execute tasks, yet she had all the prestige, money, and influence that I wanted. Thankfully, she took me under her wing and shared some things with me that I will share with you. Surprisingly, her advice emphasized the four findings I mentioned above.

Develop your personality

This means understanding what is interesting about you and putting it on display. Get clear on what makes you unique and the value your uniqueness brings to environments you are in. Once you discover that uniqueness, embody it, own it, and allow your light to shine. Shining your light doesn't belittle anyone. I've always loved the quote by Marianne Williamson about our deepest fear because it is a constant reminder that if we allow our personality to shine through, it can inspire others to be more of themselves as well. If you're not familiar with the quote, here it is: "Our deepest fear is not that we are inadequate. Our deepest fear is that we are powerful beyond measure. It is our light, not our darkness that most frightens us. We ask ourselves, Who am I to be brilliant, gorgeous, talented, fabulous? Actually, who are you not to be? You are a child of God. Your playing small does not serve the world. There is nothing enlightened about shrinking so that other people won't feel insecure around you. We are all meant to shine, as children do. We were born to make manifest the glory of God that is within us. It's not just in some of us; it's in everyone. And as we let our own light shine, we unconsciously give other people permission to do the same. As we are liberated from our own fear, our presence automatically liberates others." ~Marianne Williamson.

My first recommendation is to develop hobbies outside of work, so you will always have interesting things to talk about. It will also amplify the fun, human side of your personality. Secondly, be genuinely interested in others. Don't be afraid to ask questions to get to know people. Seek commonalities. Thirdly, stay abreast of what is going on in your company and the industry it is in. Lastly, I suggest that you read books on developing your personality.

My favorites are How to Win Friends and Influence People, Click, and Likability Factor. Developing your personality will help you become a person other people like being around, which will upgrade your perceived value and influence.

Be an effective communicator

Communication is one of the most sought-after skills in the workforce," said career expert Alison Doyle. "If you're not able to communicate effectively with co-workers, customers, or clients, you'll quickly find yourself at a disadvantage." I think it is safe to say that communication is essential. So, it will be vital for you to develop effective communication skills in the areas of speaking, writing, and other forms of media if you want to be viewed as valuable. This can make you indispensable in your current role and open opportunities to generate income outside of your job. My past career in call-center customer service served me well. It helped me learn how to control my emotions when others were irate. I became skilled at listening to what is being said and what is not said. I also learned how to convey empathy and build rapport with complete strangers. Developing these skills, as I mentioned before, was key in my transition into a new career in Instructional Design. It has also come in handy when I interview guests for my podcast, *Embrace the Upgrade*.

Another great decision I made was to join Toastmasters. Participating in this type of professional development club helped me overcome my fear of public speaking, practice the skill of communication, and become a more confident trainer. Out of all the skills I have developed, communication is the one I'm most passionate about because it allows me to share knowledge with others and build meaningful relationships. If you want to be viewed as a highly valued, indispensable addition to an organization or clients, level up your communication skills. You'll thank me later.

Embrace Negotiating

I have discovered through career coaching that many women are uncomfortable with negotiating. Much of this can be attributed to social programming and the gender norms of our culture which tell women they should be modest, and men should be competitive. This works against us when it is time for us to get what we deserve in the workplace. We don't draw attention to our accomplishments, we don't ask for raises, we don't put ourselves out there for promotions, and we do not negotiate salaries when being offered a position. According to a report by Randstad, which is a well-known staffing agency, nearly 60 percent of women never negotiate their pay. One of the blocks that prevent my clients from negotiating is confidence. Preparation will boost your confidence. Approach negotiation like you're preparing for a meeting or conversation. Focus on facts. Take emotions and neediness out of the conversation. Your goal in negotiation is to continue communicating until both sides have reached a win-win agreement. Think of it as simply a conversation. As a Get Five Certified Career Coach, I teach clients a four step-salary negotiation method that helps them quantify their worth, outshine their competition, and get the offer they want at the salary they deserve.

Here are a few negotiation tips you should remember:

- Always try to go for a win-win situation.

- Do not have a demanding or rigid attitude.

- Research the company and your industry.

- Maintain a calm, businesslike, and professional tone of voice.

- Know what you want before the negotiation begins and at what point you are willing to walk away.

- Care, but not too much. You don't want to give off a vibe of desperation. You should always have 2-3 offers you are evaluating to ensure you can genuinely have this level of confidence.

- Try to get the other party to make an offer first. If you are asked, "How much do you want?" Reply, "How much are you offering?"

Learn to Lead

It's important to know that leading is not about a title. It's about inspiring others to take action and rallying people to a cause. In essence, it is influence. How influential are you? If you increase your awareness of your personal attributes, refine your communication skills, and amplify your likability factor, you're bound to attract people to you. When you attract people to you, you want to be able to influence them to take a specific action. This can be aligned with your organization's goals and objectives, or it can be simply to do business with you. Leadership skills are in high demand, which is why you should intentionally develop this skill. It's a journey, not a destination. One of the best ways you can learn to lead is to volunteer for leadership roles on committees in your organization or a trade association in your industry. You should also read books on leadership, follow leaders who inspire you, and take notice of how they communicate. Some of my favorite leaders are Lisa

Nichols, Myron Golden, Tony Robbins, John Maxwell, Wanda Bell, and Tammy Neale. Once you've identified your ideal example, do what they do, and read what they read. If they have a blog or YouTube channel, take in their content. This will help you see things from their perspective as you take on the attributes you admire. Here's a secret, if you're drawn to a specific attribute they have, it's an indication that you already have that same attribute in you, it's just underdeveloped.

Years ago, I was in a coaching program that exposed me to this concept. I was asked who I admired most. At the time it was my director, Tammy Neale. She was such a great communicator and connected with people at all levels of the organization. She was the only Black woman on the executive leadership team which was something I had never seen before. Tammy knew how to tailor her message to the person she was talking to and was very in tune with how her message landed with the person. Once I had identified who I admired most, I was asked to look back in my life and recall times I may have done something similar. To my surprise, I thought of quite a few examples. Throughout high school, I was the go-to person for advice in my circle. Throughout college, instructors expressed appreciation for my communication skills. I even hired a communication coach, and she said she wasn't sure why I was there because I communicated very well. In college and beyond, I've always had a natural ability to connect with people from a wide variety of backgrounds. I wasn't just interested in people like me. My curiosity and appreciation for the differences in others increased my ability to connect with anyone.

The next step I had to take in the program was to send a survey out to friends and family and ask them to describe me in one word. My friends and family do not follow directions. Most of them described me in full sentences. What I noticed about their feedback was that they described me in similar ways that I described my manager. Some comments were, "Shannon is a great listener." "I like that you always give great advice." "You're always so tactful and professional." And so on. This was a huge light bulb moment and was the inspiration for me to continue to refine my communication skills. That's when I joined Toastmasters. I highly recommend you do this exercise. It's insightful and can really guide you on how to position yourself to stand out. Speaking of positioning yourself, let's get into some specific how-to's for you to follow.

How to position yourself powerfully

The first step in positioning yourself powerfully is getting to the core of who you are. What you do at your highest level reflects who you are and where you will be the most successful. If you do not know who you are and the value you bring, you cannot expect someone else to discover it. A combination of reflection, assessments, and simply paying attention to myself helped me carry out this step. It is an ongoing process because we grow and evolve constantly. When coaching clients, I take them through several exercises to jog their memory of past accomplishments, things they've done well and enjoyed. This helps them create a collection that reflects who they are. From that, they can pull keywords that describe them and use those keywords to describe their value. This works great in your resume, during interviews, and with networking.

Secondly, find what you're naturally good at. I am a natural born learner, teacher, and coach. I've always been an avid reader and remember my favorite game to play as a child was school. Being the teacher was the only choice, of course. I was a daughter of a preacher, so I taught about the Bible since I always took an insane number of notes. I really enjoyed writing. I also absorbed information quickly and could remember things easily. We had yearly Bible bees at my church when I was growing up. I won every year for my age group. Learning came easy, especially, when it was something, I was curious about. My second favorite game was to pretend I was a psychologist. My younger sister was the patient. I told her which problems she had to come to my office about and when she arrived, I'd get out my notepad and take notes while she told me her issues. Helping people solve problems felt like something I was meant to do. I have always been and still am fascinated by how the mind works, how we interpret things, and how we process information. I also love helping people become a better version of themselves. My interests and natural abilities have not changed because they are at the core of who I am.

Like me, you have stories like these. Take time to remember and document them. It will give you clues to what you do well without thinking about it. It's like you were born to do it. At this stage, don't worry how it ties into your current job or another career path. You just want to slow your mind down long enough to take notice and simply become aware of what has been there all along. I have learned that all the answers we are looking for are resting inside us, waiting for us to discover them. If we can be still long enough, we'll be amazed at what we find. So, take time to discover your own stories that hold the keys to what you were made to do. It is what you can do exceptionally well if you focus on it.

The third thing you will do is compile a list of skills you used in all the stories you discovered in the earlier step. I discovered the skills of communication, emotional intelligence, teaching, listening, writing, reading, etc. Within your stories are a treasure trove of undiscovered skills and talents just waiting to be revealed. List everything that comes to mind. Don't leave anything out. Don't second guess anything. The point of this exercise is to get everything out of your head and onto paper. Next, look at the list and highlight the skills you enjoy most. Then find ways to creatively describe yourself based on those skills. You may be a marketing maven or a provocative intellectual or a laser-focused listener. You can use these descriptors along with your area of focus to introduce yourself in networking events and on social media profiles such as LinkedIn. I do much more detailed work with coaching clients in this step using a precise science that has seen phenomenal results. From here, you want to focus on your marketability which may require that you add a few other skills to your repertoire. In the next chapter, we will take what you have discovered here and get crystal clear on what you want in your career!

CHAPTER 7:

DEVELOP A CAREER ASCENSION ROADMAP

"If you fail to plan, you are planning to fail."
— Benjamin Franklin

Where are you going professionally? Now is the time to get in the driver's seat of your career! When you're passive, you're in the passenger seat. Someone else is deciding the direction of your work and life. I believe it's important to have a career ascension roadmap (car). This roadmap is the vehicle that will take you where you want to go in your career whether that is a leadership role or starting your own business.

A successful career requires you to proactively plan and manage it. Before managing your new career, you must develop a roadmap to your desired destination and detail how you are going to get there. Your career ascension roadmap will be an action plan that outlines:

1. **Where you are now** - including job title, income, tasks, projects, etc.

2. **Where you want to be** - including future employment or entrepreneurship, income, titles, tasks, projects, etc.

3. **The gaps or obstacles in your way** - do you lack skills, connections, experience, etc.?

4. The route you intend to take to overcome obstacles, close gaps, and reach your destination.

To create your career ascension roadmap, you will need to implement five simple steps.

Step One: Identify where you are in your career.

Look at your current position. Do you enjoy it? If not, why not? Have you developed skills you believe are valuable? Think about the tasks you enjoy doing. What about your career, if anything, makes you look forward to getting up each morning? What are your strengths and weaknesses? Be sure to refer to what you have learned about yourself in the self-discovery phase, too. In addition, consider all your job experiences and identify what energized you versus drained you in each role.

Step Two: Start thinking about where you want to go.

Now comes the fun part. Visualize where you would rather be. This is not the time to be "realistic" or "practical". Let your imagination run wild and capture what's in your heart on paper. Think about what type of job titles, tasks, responsibilities, industries, and companies appeal to you. To avoid being overwhelmed by looking too far ahead, consider only looking ahead for the next one to three years. If you're comfortable looking further ahead, by all means do so! The one-to-three-year time frame is close enough to your current day-to-day job which makes it easier to visualize your goals for your next step.

Step Three: Find the gap between your current position and your dream position.

This process is called a gap analysis. To complete a gap analysis, you will need to research your ideal career path. I used bls.gov,

job search sites, onetonline.gov, careeronestop.org and myskillsmyfuture.org. After conducting research, it is common to find that you don't have all the required skills you need for your chosen career path. Don't be discouraged! This is what you would call a skill gap. You may also have gaps in your knowledge or experience, and that is ok. There are a host of free online learning resources such as Coursera and MIT OpenCourseware to close knowledge or skill gaps. Volunteering is an excellent way to close experience gaps.

Next, find three to five job descriptions that represent the type of position you want to have in the next one to three years. Once you have identified your 2-3 job descriptions, it is time to conduct informational interviews. Informational interviews are a vital part of your research.

Remember when I shared the story earlier about how I reached out to the instructional designers at my job and conducted interviews on my lunch break for months? This was the point in my process that I conducted that series of interviews.

Here are a few questions I used:

- What do you enjoy most and least about the work you do?

- How did you get into this role?

- What do you think are the most important skills to have to succeed in this role?

- Do you have any recommendations for other people I should talk to or other resources I should explore?

I also asked each person if they would mind if we kept in contact so I could update them on my progress. Not only will you gather valuable information during informational interviews, asking this last question helps you expand your network. You will discover that those who you interview will feel invested in your journey if you keep in contact. Once you've reviewed the information you've gathered from researching your ideal roles and the interviews, list the skills and other qualifications you need to make the shift. As you review the list, look at both the skills you have as well as those you don't have. Then focus on developing the skills you lack to close gaps. Reference the skill building chapter on how to execute this step.

Step Four: Create your C.A.R. (Career Ascension Roadmap)

This plan should include all the information you have gathered up to this point. You will also add the next role after your target role, so you have something to look forward to after your current goal is reached. You should never stagnate or be complacent in your career. That's the fast track to passive town and we don't live there anymore, right? It should also include a list of skills, education, and experiences you want to gain over the next few years and concrete steps you will take to obtain those skills, education, or experience. You will need to review this document twice per year to monitor your progress and ensure you are moving in the right direction.

Having a coach, accountability partner, or mentor is extremely helpful to keep you on track. Be sure to address any behaviors and thoughts that undermine your progress and maximize the behaviors that lead to successful outcomes. If you take all the necessary action steps, you will eventually land the role you desire. When you do (it's only a matter of when), you will want to have a plan in place to proactively manage your career while planning your future progression. Never get too comfortable in a role, always look toward what is next for you!

HOW TO PROACTIVELY MANAGE YOUR CAREER

To proactively manage your career, you need to take control of your destiny. You can do this by taking some key steps, such as:

1. **Knowing what you want** - This may seem like an obvious step, but many people don't take the time to figure out what they truly want in a career. They may be swayed by what others tell them they should do, or by their current job situation. But if you want to be proactive about your career, you need to know what you want and where you see yourself in the future.

2. **Planning and goal setting** - Once you know what you want, you need to start planning how to get there. This includes setting specific goals and developing a roadmap (your C.A.R.) on how to achieve them. Having a plan will give you the focus and motivation you need to stay on track and make progress toward your ultimate goal.

3. **Taking action** - It's not enough to just have a plan or know what you want. You also need to take action and put that plan into action. This means making a commitment to yourself and following through with it, no matter what challenges or obstacles come up along the way.

4. **Learning and growth** - A key part of managing your career is ongoing learning and growth. You need to be constantly expanding your skillset and knowledge in order to stay ahead of the curve and be successful in whatever field you choose. So, make sure that learning is a key part of your overall strategy for career success. If you want to be proactive about your career, these are some of the steps you need to take. With dedication and commitment, you can achieve anything you set your mind to!

Transitioning from career frustration to career elevation requires time, effort, and patience. It also requires moving out of your comfort zone. However, if you are committed to your goals, there is no reason you should not be able to achieve what you desire. Reflecting on who you are and what drives you will help center your career goals. This will also help you create more meaningful connections that will make the most of your skills and strengths. The activities mentioned in the chapters of this book are designed to help you clarify and reinforce your professional values, goals, and guide you towards a fulfilling career. If you have followed the steps I outlined in this book, you will have built a solid foundation for a successful career. If you are still floundering, go back and start again. Remember, nothing will work unless you do, and it is never too late for an upgrade!

At this point, you have upgraded your thinking, achieved greater self-awareness, and have upgraded your personal brand, skills, and network. Now it's time to use this progress to consider all your career options, including ways to create streams of income outside of your job. Having one source of income is risky. Anything could happen to us at any time. Statistics show that many Americans are only one paycheck away from financial ruin. Having an alternate income source would certainly have eliminated much of the suffering and struggles I endured as a single mom ten plus years ago. I want to share some ideas that can help you upgrade from one income stream to as many as you'd like! So, keep reading to discover them in the next chapter.

CHAPTER 8:

EVALUATE YOUR CAREER OPTIONS

If don't find a way to make money while you sleep, you will work until you die."
— Warren Buffett

So, you have your C.A.R. in place and are closer to career elevation, congrats! Now you want to rise above the financial risk of having only one source of income by exploring other income options. The only challenge is, you don't know where to start! Don't worry my friend, I thought about that and have dedicated a whole chapter to sharing various traditional and non-traditional career options for you to consider.

CAREER OPTIONS

There are seasons where employment is necessary even if you have ambitions for entrepreneurship. In my opinion, until you're able to be the CEO of your career, you will not be ready to be the CEO of your own company. That may not be a popular opinion, yet I stand by it, nonetheless. You will need to start thinking like an entrepreneur while working if you want to upgrade to become the CEO of your business.

How to think like an entrepreneur at work

So, how do you think like an entrepreneur on a job? Thinking like an entrepreneur while being an employee is all about having the right mindset. You need to be creative and think outside the box, look for ways to improve your skills and advance your career. You also need to be proactive, instead of waiting for someone else to give you a promotion or raise. What I consider most important is being passionate and committed to your work while putting your best foot forward. If you can successfully adopt these attitudes and behaviors, you'll be well on your way to thinking like an entrepreneur at work. There are seven additional things that I suggest you do:

- See your employer as your client.

- Resist the need to be perfect and focus on action/ results.

- View your work as a portfolio of your skills and abilities.

- Develop your ability to control your emotions and doubts.

- Volunteer to take on roles or tasks before you think you are ready if they will help you to develop a needed skill.

- Find 2-3 people who you trust that can hold you accountable for achieving your goals.

- Increase your ability to bounce back from setbacks, delays, or negative outcomes.

Take time to discover what made your employer choose you over other candidates. Find out what results you get that are valued, what needs are you addressing with your skills, and what characteristics, strengths, or abilities that are appreciated. The perfect time to ask these questions is during performance reviews and one-on-one meetings with your manager. Once you've collected this information, you can then come up with ways to communicate that value in the marketplace to sell products or services that will utilize the same skills you use at work. If those skills are valuable to your employer, they'll be valuable to other organizations and/or clients as well.

On the other hand, if you do not have aspirations of being in business for yourself, you shouldn't feel bad about that, no matter what the internet, influencers or business coaches say. Instead, you can adopt an entrepreneurial mindset in your career and use different strategies to add additional income to your household. This will allow you to live comfortably and avoid financial vulnerability. It is important for you to understand that it is essential to have an income stream outside of your job. Relying solely on your job for income is risky. Research from the Federal Reserve found that 4 in 10 Americans couldn't afford a $ 400 emergency, and 22 % say they expect to have to miss payments on some of their bills. I have included a list of 25 ways to generate income outside of your job. With these 25 different side hustles to choose from, you can take some time to test some out and find the right one for you. The great thing about most of these options is the flexibility they offer. In most cases, you can work whatever hours you want, and put in as many or as few hours as you need based on your schedule. The other benefit of trying side hustles while working is that you can use this to discover new passions and interests that could possibly turn into a full-time career or business. Take this time to accept that there are literally no limits other than the ones you place on yourself. People have created lucrative income streams out of the most unlikely things such as being paid to manage the Facebook accounts of people who have passed away, doggie daycare, selling friendship, and reviewing sensitive content for Google. So, if they can do it, so can you.

Side Hustle Ideas

Here are the 25 ways to generate income outside your job as a starting point to open your eyes to possibilities you may not have considered. I'd also love to hear from you on other ways you may have discovered as well! Feel free to follow Embrace the Upgrade on Facebook and share your other ideas!

Side Hustle #1: Get Hired to Handle Tasks for Others

Becoming a virtual assistant is just like being an assistant or secretary for a client at an office, except your office is now your home. As more jobs become remote, assistants are needed. Businesses and even solo entrepreneurs still need someone to answer calls, plan out schedules, and do the more common tasks they don't always have time for. You may find yourself doing tasks like answering emails with a script, double-checking stored information, and processing simple data. Some virtual assistants focus primarily on the social media aspect of a brand.

This includes creating and posting blog posts, TikTok's, editing YouTube videos, and creating content that will help promote the brand or client you are working with. One of the best aspects of virtual assisting is the ability to work with your client to set your own hours and wages. Being a virtual assistant can become a full-time job, but it all depends on who you end up working for, and what they need from you.

Side Hustle #2: Narrate for Audiobooks

Some avid readers don't have the time to sit down and read a book. So many people are turning to audiobooks so they can multitask and enjoy content while getting their work done. As audiobooks continue to grow in popularity, more and more self-published authors are searching to find the perfect voice for their books. If you enjoy acting and speaking, narrating is a great path to take. All you need is a quiet studio to work in, which you can create in your own home.

Once you have a solid setup, you can begin recording some samples to put in your portfolio. These could be simple recordings of you reading pages from some of your favorite books. Try to include different genres to show your range of emotion and inflection. To create a home studio, you just need a quiet spot with lots of items to deflect the bounce of sound and prevent echoes. There are even tabletop acoustic foam sets you can use to absorb the echo and help your narration come out sounding polished to perfection!

Side Hustle #2: Become a Ghostwriter

There are plenty of opportunities for anyone who wants to become a ghostwriter. As a ghostwriter, you are simply given the job of writing the content that other people either don't want to write or don't have the time to write. You will be given a task with an outline or summary that gives you an idea of what you must write. Then it is up to you to fulfill your client's vision. Many different types of content are available for ghostwriters. You could be writing content for emails, websites, blog posts, eBooks, social media posts, press releases, and more.

Brands trust you to write in a professional voice, since your writing will reflect on the brand. Try writing a few samples so you don't have an empty portfolio. These can be basic ideas, but they should show off how you write in terms of quality and style. Once you have a few things in your portfolio, you can sign up for freelance platforms. Upwork and Fiverr are typically the most popular options for ghostwriters. Make sure to include as much information as you can on your profile. This should include how much you want to be paid, what types of ghostwriting jobs you are searching for, and your experience and education. Once your profile is set up, you can start applying for listed jobs that fit your interests and skills. You can also launch your own ghostwriting website to get direct jobs, so the platforms don't take a cut, and you'll begin getting jobs as positive word of mouth spreads about your quality.

Side Hustle #3: Participate in Focus Groups

There is always new research to be done when it comes to marketing and understanding the way a human's mind works. Companies will create surveys and other methods for businesses so that they can sell their research to businesses and brands looking for marketing research. These companies are always looking for people who are willing to participate in focus groups. You can apply to join and, if accepted, you can get paid either per project or per hour. Make sure to only sign up for paid focus groups. It is important to make sure you are qualified for the focus group you want to join. Some of this research will target certain demographics, so make sure to read the requirements ahead of time. Sometimes, they will have you fill out a pre-survey, so you know for sure whether you qualify. They may even interview you beforehand to see if you're a good fit, and that may include asking you things like how old you are, what race or political affiliation you belong to, and so on.

Side Hustle #4: Manage a Brand or Influencer's Social Media

To make the most of one's influence and following, creators post on every social media app possible to optimize their reach. This is especially important when an influencer wants to create merchandise or go on tour. Managing every social media post and creating all that content can take up a lot of time and energy. That's where you come in. As a social media manager, you help influencers create exciting and engaging content for all their social media pages. You can help with profile changes, managing what content should go out and when it should be posted, designing fun Instagram stories, and just assisting your client with any social media needs.

Side Hustle #5: Edit YouTube and TikTok Videos

Video content has grown more popular recently, which is mainly due to TikTok's rise in popularity. A lot of creators gain their influence by frequently posting on YouTube and TikTok. Video content allows influencers to show more emotion and passion, while also showcasing different niches, like fashion or DIYs. Once your client has pressed record and created some videos, it is up to you to edit and polish them so that each video is appealing and runs smoothly. You may have to edit out pauses in your client's talking, and any other noises that may interrupt things. You may need to find good background music and add aesthetic text to go with each video, depending on what your client wants. There are plenty of video editing tools you can choose to download, and some are even free. Before you start applying for these jobs, you may want to consider messing around on the apps you use to ensure you are fully experienced and prepared. If your customer allows it, you may even be able to provide contact information for your services at the end of a video, or in its description. This is a great way to show off your work and gain potential customers.

Side Hustle #6: Become a Freelance Graphic Designer

Visuals are a major part of any marketing. How a brand is designed can have a significant effect on whether potential customers become confirmed buyers. People need graphic designers for logos, website design, posts, headers and banners, advertisements, and even covers for their eBooks. Some businesses require some type of college degree when hiring, but many do not – and you can put up gigs as a freelancer where you're not working for anyone else but yourself. As long as you can show examples of your work to prospective clients and you understand the project, you can make quite the business for yourself.

Before applying for graphic design gigs, make sure to have a full portfolio. In your portfolio, include logo designs, random illustrations, and creative social media templates. Having a wide variety of creations in your portfolio will help potential customers get an idea of your creativity and artistic style.

Side Hustle #7: Create an Online Thrift Shop

Thrifting has become a popular trend for many ages. As more people are beginning to express their personalized fashion sense online, they are looking for unique finds that will help them stand out. You can go thrifting to find amazing vintage pieces for a small amount of money. Goodwill, Savers, and the Salvation Army are some of the more trusted thrift stores. You can even go searching for garage sales to find unique pieces for incredibly low prices.

Once you know what to look for, you can turn those pieces into profit by selling them online. You can sell these clothing items on sites like Facebook Marketplace, Depop, Poshmark, and eBay. You can even take some of these items and flip them with your own creativity. If you know how to sew, or even embroider, you can add small touches to make them special or personalized.

Side Hustle #8: Become a Freelance Editor

If grammar and punctuation come easily to you, becoming a freelance editor is a great way to make some extra money on the side. Many entrepreneurs can write out their own thoughts and ideas, but don't always know how to make things grammatically correct. Some writers even struggle with making their writing more exciting by using a wider variety of words. You can apply for editing jobs on freelance sites like Upwork and Fiverr. Many self-publishing authors just want to hire an editor to go over their work before they publish their eBooks. It may seem like tedious work, but you can earn a solid payout if your editing becomes reputable.

Side Hustle #9: List Anything Online Before Donating

If you find yourself doing some cleaning up and end up with a pile of things to get rid of, consider listing those items online before you drop them off at your local Goodwill. You may not expect most of it to sell, but you might be surprised by the things people are willing to buy secondhand. If you have any family members or friends who are also getting rid of random things, consider asking them to drop them off at your house instead. You can create your own miniature store with different items. You can try to sell these items on Facebook Marketplace, eBay, and even Craigslist. These include things like clothes, shoes, electronics, books, fitness gear, and more.

Side Hustle #10: Sell Printables on Etsy

Printables are common on Etsy due to the wide variety of possible printable niches to create with. When you find your target audience and learn about the kind of content they want to purchase, you will be able to get creative with making as many different printables as possible for the audience. You can create templates for planners, calendars, checklists, weight loss trackers, worksheets, wedding shower games, questionnaires, and itineraries. You can create individual listings for each template you make so customers can purchase a downloadable digital file of your work. This takes out the shipping step, so you don't have as much to do when someone makes a purchase. You can even bundle some of your printables to bring in higher sales.

Side Hustle #11: Become a Stock Photographer

Whenever a blogger, brand, or entrepreneur is creating content, they will usually go to a stock photo site for photos rather than hiring a personal photographer. These stock photo sites are constantly looking for photographers to buy photos from. If you have an eye for good photos, you can sell your images to these sites and collect a payout every time someone downloads your image on their site. You can do this on sites like iStock Photo, Pexels, and Shutterstock. Once you submit a photo and it is accepted, it will be published publicly for commercial use. It is important to make sure your photos qualify with the submission guidelines and rules. When you are taking photos, try to keep in mind what the public wants. Find a niche and take many photos for that niche so there is a wide selection. For example, if you want to provide photos for a fitness blog or brand, take photos of someone tying their shoes, or unbranded dumbbells sitting on a table, or an exercise ball sitting on a yoga mat.

Side Hustle #12: Create Online Courses for a Specific Niche

Holding information can be more powerful than many people know. If you are well-informed on any niche topic, you can use that knowledge to your advantage. People are always looking to learn more and improve their interests and skills. You can share your knowledge with the world and make a profit from it by offering paid online courses, eBooks, and training sessions. It will take time, and you have to make sure your content looks professional and is accurate, but you can generate revenue with the information that is already in your brain. You can create books and courses on many different topics. For example, if you love fitness, you could record videos that include your favorite exercise routines. You could also offer training sessions over Zoom with a smaller crowd of people to encourage a community. You can build a loyal community of followers who view you as a trustworthy teacher, which means they will have no problem recommending you to people they know and buying your future products as they are released.

Side Hustle #13: Become an Online Tutor for Children

Parents are some of the busiest people in the world, take it from a mom of four. If their kids are struggling with grades, they may not be available to give them proper help and guidance. Paying for a tutor to come to the house every night may also be too costly. You can offer your tutoring services online for any specific topics you feel most confident in. Many websites require some kind of degree or credentials, but some will let you take a few classes to get certified. You can also freelance, and post service offers on other freelance sites. You can help with many different subjects and grade levels – from reading for an elementary school child to calculus for a high school student.

Side Hustle #14: Become a Product Blogger

Creating your own blog gives you the freedom to write about anything that interests you. Passionate writing draws in an audience because people will believe you are sincere with your work and recommendations. To have a successful blog, you have to be willing to post frequently, and spend time making your posts informative and helpful for readers. Recommending products means you must fully believe that the product you are writing about is a quality item. You can bring in revenue as an affiliate blogger by linking to Amazon and other platforms every time you talk about a product. If your blog becomes successful, you can even allow ads and make extra money off that option as well. Affiliate blogging can be done for both digital and tangible products. So, if you go into a niche like Survival Prepping, you might promote info product courses on Click Bank as well as survival gear on Amazon.

Side Hustle #15: Get Paid for Your Online Presence

If you are an interesting person, have interesting stories, have passion for a specific niche, or have a talent to show off, you can build a name for yourself just by posting online. Social media plays a hand in the careers of most people who thrive off a loyal audience. Becoming popular on social media allows you to influence a large group of people. This means that brands and businesses will be willing to pay you money to show off their products. Brand deals can bring in a solid amount of money, and all you have to do is talk about their products. You can become a social media influencer regardless of what your original topic was. All it takes is the ability to gain followers and get engagement and a variety of brands will approach you in an effort to get exposure to your following.

Side Hustle #16: Notarize Important Documents for Others

Becoming a notary public and only doing online work allows you to work from the comfort of your home, all while choosing your own active hours. Before putting your name out there, you will have to apply to become a notary, which involves paying some state fees. This job will involve many files being shared back and forth so you can verify your client's identity. Once you have all the information you need, you will need to have some sort of video call of you signing the right files, so they can witness your signature for legal purposes. Then you can send the necessary files back to your client and receive your pay. Utilizing freelance websites may be the safest way to set up contracts with your clients to avoid any issues.

Side Hustle #17: Sell Domains to Interested Parties

Some domains have been sitting unused for years – or have recently expired and the owner forgot to renew its registration. If you can buy up those domains and resell them for a profit, you'll be able to build your own domain flipping business. For some domains you can take the time to design the website so that it is visually appealing to any potential buyers. You can even work to push your domains to rank highly on search engines so that customers will be incentivized to purchase that domain. You can set a flat price on the domain name or put it up for auction to see how high the bids will go. You can also bundle up a set of domains to brands who may want to maximize their reach using a variety of keywords.

Side Hustle #18: Create Audio Content for a Specific Niche

You can gain influence in the social media world (and get paid for it) without ever showing your face. The important thing is what you have to say, and how you say it. You can create a podcast, like Upgrade to Get Paid, by focusing on a popular niche you can talk about for a significant amount of time – about 20 minutes or more in one sitting. You can post podcasts online for free on sites like Buzzsprout, Spreaker, and Podbean. Then, you can get paid for including ads on your podcast episodes, depending on the number of listeners you get. Some brands will reach out to you personally to work out an agreement and sponsor your podcast. Some of the more professional podcasts have expensive microphones and equipment. If you are starting on a lower budget, you can just use your phone to record if you are in a quiet space. As you continue to grow, you can upgrade your equipment in increments.

Side Hustle #19: Become a Product Tester

When products are created, they must be tested by a group of people before being made public so the business can ensure there are no issues with the product. You can provide an outsider's opinion and test the quality of a company's product. There are several product testing job sites available with one simple search. You may have to fill out a survey or take a test to see if you qualify for their target demographic. Once you are accepted, they will ship the product to you so you can test and review it. You're a paid participant, but you must commit to the entirety of the testing opportunity.

Side Hustle #20: Launch Your Own Online Store

If you are good at noticing product trends and you can usually guess what will sell, you may want to consider launching your own eCommerce site. You can invest in various products, build up a stock, and sell various products from your own shop. If you include popular trending products in your store and are able to reach an online audience, you can send buyers right to your site where they find other products to purchase as well. You can buy a large amount of these products for a discount from wholesalers which lets you earn a profit when you sell the products for a higher price. Look for programs like Amazon's FBA (Fulfilled By Amazon) system. You'll find products and have them shipped directly to their warehouse, so that when and if they sell, Amazon can pack it up and ship it straight to your customer on your behalf.

Side Hustle #21: Create a Drop shipping Store

If you know how to draw in an audience and drive traffic to a storefront, this is a great side hustle to try. The idea focuses on you being the messenger that connects consumers to products. You can create posts on social media about a product and promote it to your viewers. Once they go to your storefront and make a purchase, you then forward the orders to the business or brand you are working for. You get to keep a portion of the profit for yourself, which is where you generate an income. This process works similarly to affiliate marketing with an Amazon storefront. The only difference is that you will be working with different businesses and brands. Choose a specific niche so that all your products will have something in common and be of interest to potential customers. For example, you might have a wedding storefront, or a beauty niche drop shipping business.

Side Hustle #22: Become a Remote English Educator

There are many people around the world who don't have access to an in-person English speaking teacher. When people are preparing to travel, they often go online to learn the language of the place they are traveling to. You can find sites that will connect you to potential students looking for English teachers. You can then become a tutor online, teaching English to those who have yet to learn the language. You might work one on one with a student, or in a group setting. You'll be helping them master the English language with lesson plans and homework. If you know a second language such as French, Chinese, or another language so you can communicate with the students, that's even better!

Side Hustle #23: Become an Independent Author

There is an endless number of avid readers in the world who are always looking for new books to digest. If you like to write, you can turn it into a career by starting out publishing just one book. You can write your own book in any genre and publish it independently. Whatever platform you use may take a percentage of each sale. If you choose a popular niche to write your book about, it will be much easier to gain sales and make an actual profit. Some people write non-fiction books such as how to survive in the wilderness. Others prefer to write fiction novels about romance, sci-fi, mystery, and more. You can do a combination of these as well and just use separate pen names!

Side Hustle #24: Design and Sell Printed Products

You can sell print on demand products that you've designed as a side hustle. You can create designs and have bigger companies print them out as you sell your designs to consumers. These creations can be placed on shirts, hoodies, stickers, coffee mugs, and patches. You can come up with many different logos, quotes, and other designs that will be aesthetically pleasing to possible customers.

Side Hustle #25: Rent Out Something You Own

If you have something someone else needs to use, you can now find ways to be a landlord of sorts. Even if it's not property that you're renting out, you can start a side hustle where you rent things by the hour, day, or weeks. People are using apps and sites to rent out their belongings. For example, if your home has a swimming pool, you can charge by the hour for people to rent it. Some people may want to have a get together in your backyard or just relax in private without being at a public pool. If you don't mind people coming inside, you can also rent out your kitchen. Many people who host cooking classes in larger kitchens or who even rent your dining room along with it for an elegant meal cooked by a chef. You can rent out other things, too, such as your car or boat. This is big business in many areas, and the nicer your car or boat, the more you can charge for people to rent it. You can even rent out gadgets like lawn equipment. Lawnmowers are expensive and require upkeep, so many find themselves in a pinch and need to mow their lawn before they receive a citation. You can rent out camping gear and even chicken coops if you want to! These are perfect side hustles for those who aren't using their belongings very often and who want to make money on the side from what they own. You'll still be in total control over the situation, specifying the rate and how far people are allowed to take the item. You get paid directly from the app as soon as your rental is returned to you. People will even rent garden space from you. If you have a backyard with soil, sun, and shade, consider letting people grow their vegetables and herbs in it. This can be a situation where you receive fresh produce as payment, taking the pressure off you of worrying where money for food will come from during an inflationary period. You can also rent your backyard out to dog owners who need to let their four-legged friend run around, but who don't want to go to a public dog park and risk their pet getting attacked or catching a disease.

There's no end to the many side hustles you can choose from. All you have to do is test a few and see how well it works and how much you enjoy it. Or you can create your own from your existing skills!

CHAPTER 9:

LET'S SUM IT ALL UP

"All good things must come to an end"
– Jim Geoffrey Chaucer

There is a lot to take in and consider in these pages. Throughout this book, you've learned how vital it is to shift from passive to powerful so you can shift from career frustration to career elevation. You've also gained a new perspective on why we must update our programming so we can take on new beliefs and experience affirming emotions. You've discovered the value of prioritizing skill building and mastery so you can stay in demand and earn what you deserve. You now know who should be in your power circle so you will always be inspired to be your best self and how to create a plan that will help you shift into a career you love.

Not only that, but you also have twenty-five options to create additional income streams, so you don't have to rely solely on your job! I think we can both agree that there's much to be done and think about. For now, just pause and breathe. Resist the urge to rush to do all the things you read about. This journey you are on is a marathon, not a sprint, and you're the only one on the track. You're not in competition with anyone other than the last version of you. So, relieve yourself of any pressure and simply be in this moment. I want you to take a step back and acknowledge how far you've come. Celebrate even the smallest milestones. Hey, you've read this entire book! Woo Hoo!

Take your time and implement at a pace that works for you. I want you to start paying attention to how your thinking changes and write about it in your journal. Notice where you may feel anticipation or excitement. Discern where you may feel uncertainty or anxiety. Pay attention and listen to yourself. Remember to write down those aha moments, doing so will help you build greater self-awareness. I remember a business coach telling me to slow down to go fast. I used to feel like my mind was always racing. Ideas come to me so quickly and it seemed like I was always in problem solving mode. I appreciated that advice so much and since then, I have never been the same. So, I am going to encourage you to do the same. Resist the urge to be in a hurry. Take time to enjoy this process and journey of becoming a new version of yourself. It is the best form of personal development I have ever experienced. You are literally transforming into a whole new identity and shedding an old one. You're leaving behind the existence of passively accepting whatever life throws your way, to become a person of power and intention who creates the type of career and life they want. You're saying goodbye to leasing your life. Now you own it. It's a powerful transition. Think of this period of time as a form of metamorphosis. I want to share some things that have helped me along the way and continue to help me as I continue on this journey with you.

TIPS FOR ENJOYING THE JOURNEY

Make time for laughter

I can't emphasize enough the importance of infusing joy into this very noble journey you've embarked upon. There's enough serious business in your career, so you must make time for laughter. There are many benefits of laughter such as stress relief, boosts to your immune system, stimulation of your organs, improvement to your mood, and an increase in your sense of well-being. I love the fact that as a mom I have kiddos who have plenty of corny jokes to crack me up. If you're a parent, you know what I mean. If you aren't a parent, watch comedy shows (Kevin Hart is my fav), hang out with friends or family, or fake laugh until it becomes real (it actually works!) All in all, the point is to find joy, so go out and get a good laugh or two today!

Create a career you can enjoy

When you are deciding on your ideal career, don't forget to create a career you will look forward to working in. Think about what types of people you want to work with. What type of tasks energize you? Infuse those things in your career so when times get challenging, you'll still enjoy the work you do.

Become someone you admire

Becoming someone, you admire is one of the greatest gifts you can give to yourself. After all, you carry yourself everywhere you go, you should at least like you. For years, I couldn't look myself in the mirror because I disliked myself to that degree. Over time, with much therapy, personal development, and healthy relationships, I've evolved into someone I admire. I appreciate my strength, courage, resilience, work ethic, compassion, and adaptability. Do yourself a favor, invest in yourself so you can admire yourself. You won't regret it!

Take one day at a time

As the saying goes, Rome wasn't built in one day. Your career transformation will not happen in a day either. Accepting this fact should take unnecessary pressure off of you and help you focus on one day at a time. Sure, you need to be focused, consistent, and all the productive things, but you also need to only do what you can do with the present and allow the rest to take care of itself. It's all about balance and perspective.

My friend, it has been such a pleasure sharing with you in this book. I hope you've enjoyed it and have learned a lot. Consider this a reference guide and review it as much as you need. The great thing about this book is that I wrote it in a way that allows you to go straight to the chapter you need help with most and focus only on that until you are ready to move on. Sending you much love and warm wishes on your journey as you become the powerful and wholeheartedly fulfilled person I know you can be!

CHAPTER 10:

WHAT'S NEXT

It is always your next move.
– Napoleon Hill

Now that you're done reading the book, you may be thinking you need help to implement what you have read. Don't worry, my friend, I've already thought of that and have your next steps planned out. You've probably noticed that throughout the book, I've mentioned courses and coaching. I have an amazing opportunity for you to do a deep dive with me to implement everything you've learned in this book.

The Empowered to Upgrade Coaching Program

Empowered to Upgrade offers a deeper dive into the concepts shared in this book. You will have an opportunity to have a HR Certified Trainer and Certified Career Coach to walk you through each phase of the UPGRADE method step-by-step. If you're ready to take control of your career and start living a life you love, apply to enroll in this 6-week career transition intensive today.

In this program, you'll receive the tools, roadmap, and confidence to pursue a new role or industry so you can finally love what you do, and look forward to Monday mornings, too. Don't wait – your dream career is waiting for you! Visit shannondsmith.com for more information.

MEET YOUR CAREER STRATEGIST

f you're feeling frustrated in your career, Shannon is the one you need to call! She is a multi-passionate Career Strategist and Personal Effectiveness Trainer. She is living proof that it is never too late to upgrade! Shannon will help you shine and discover new opportunities. She partners with clients to develop personalized action plans that get them what they want from their careers, as well as overcome any challenges or obstacles in the process for sustainable results! She chose this work because she know how hard it can be when are you stuck in a career that doesn't make you happy. Her work is accomplished by addressing mindset, skillset, and strategies to achieve career alignment. Shannon has a unique perspective because she transformed her career after divorce and continues to expand her capabilities daily. You can learn more about Shannon at shannondsmith.com

LOVED THE BOOK?

Don't forget to leave a review! Every review matter, and it matters a *lot!* Head over to Amazon or wherever you purchased this book to leave an honest review for me. I thank you from the bottom of my heart!

9 798218 091897